SORRENTO

TRAVEL GUIDE 2024 AND BEYOND

A Journey Through Culture, Hidden Gems, Cuisine and Local Secrets in the Metropolitan City of Naples, Italy – Packed with Detailed Maps & Itinerary Planner

BY

JAMES W. PATRICK

Copyright © 2024 by James W. Patrick. All rights reserved. The content of this work, including but not limited to text, images, and other media, is owned by James W. Patrick and is protected under copyright laws and international agreements. No part of this work may be reproduced, shared, or transmitted in any form or by any means without the explicit written consent of James W. Patrick. Unauthorized use, duplication, or distribution of this material may lead to legal action, including both civil and criminal penalties. For permission requests or further inquiries, please reach out to the author via the contact details provided in the book or on the author's official page.

TABLE OF CONTENTS

Copyright... 1
My Experience in Sorrento... 5
Sorrento FAQ?.. 7
Why Visit Sorrento?.. 10
What to Expect from this Guide... 12

CHAPTER 1 INTRODUCTION TO SORRENTO.. 15
1.1. Overview of Sorrento... 15
1.2. History and Significance.. 17
1.3. Geography and Climate... 19
1.4. Local Customs and Traditions... 20
1.5. Best Times to Visit... 22

CHAPTER 2 ACCOMMODATION OPTIONS.. 24
2.1. Luxury Hotels and Resorts.. 24
2.2. Mid-Range and Budget Hotels.. 26
2.3. Bed and Breakfasts and Guesthouses.. 28
2.4. Self-Catering Apartments and Villas... 30
2.5. Hostels and Affordable Accommodations.. 32

CHAPTER 3 TRANSPORTATION IN SORRENTO.. 35
3.1. Getting to Sorrento: Air, Train, and Road Options................................... 35
3.2. Public Transportation: Buses and Taxis.. 37
3.3. Walking and Scooter Rentals.. 39
3.4. Ferries and Boat Transfers.. 41
3.5. Accessibility for Disabled Travelers... 43

CHAPTER 4 TOP ATTRACTIONS.. 45
4.1. Sorrento Historic Center and Piazza Tasso.. 45
4.2. Marina Grande and Fishing Harbor... 48
4.3. Cathedral of Sorrento and Religious Sites.. 50
4.4. Museo Correale and Art Galleries... 52

4.5. Villa Comunale and Panoramic Views..58

CHAPTER 5 PRACTICAL INFORMATION AND TRAVEL RESOURCES..................61
5.1 Maps and Navigation...61
5.2 Essential Packing List..63
5.3 Visa Requirements and Entry Procedures..65
5.4 Safety Tips and Emergency Contacts...68
5.5 Currency, Banking, Budgeting and Money Matters..70
5.6 Language, Communication and Useful Phrases..73
5.7 Useful Websites, Mobile Apps and Online Resources.....................................76
5.8 Visitor Centers and Tourist Assistance...79

CHAPTER 6 CULINARY DELIGHTS...82
6.1. Traditional Italian and Sorrentine Cuisine...82
6.2. Seafood Restaurants and Pizzerias...84
6.3. Cafes and Gelaterias..87
6.4. Local Wine and Limoncello Tasting...89
6.5. Cooking Classes and Culinary Tours...92

CHAPTER 7 CULTURE AND HERITAGE..95
7.1. Historical Buildings and Architecture...95
7.2. Music and Performing Arts...98
7.3. Festivals and Cultural Events...101
7.4. Crafts and Local Artisans...104
7.5. Literary and Historical Figures...107

CHAPTER 8 OUTDOOR ACTIVITIES AND ADVENTURES...................................110
8.1. Hiking and Nature Trails...110
8.2. Water Sports and Beach Activities...112
8.3. Boat Tours and Cruises..115
8.4. Diving and Snorkeling...117
8.5. Gardens and Parks...120
8.6 Family and Kids Friendly Activities..122
8.7 Activities for Solo Travelers...125

CHAPTER 9 SHOPPING IN SORRENTO ... 128
- 9.1. Boutiques and Fashion Stores ... 128
- 9.2. Souvenir Shops and Local Crafts ... 130
- 9.3. Art Galleries and Antique Dealers ... 133
- 9.4. Food Markets and Specialty Shops ... 136
- 9.5. Shopping Streets and Centers ... 138

CHAPTER 10 DAY TRIPS AND EXCURSIONS ... 141
- 10.1. Capri and the Blue Grotto ... 141
- 10.2. Amalfi Coast and Positano ... 142
- 10.3. Pompeii and Herculaneum ... 144
- 10.4. Naples and Its Attractions ... 146
- 10.5. Ischia and Thermal Spas ... 148

CHAPTER 11 ENTERTAINMENT AND NIGHTLIFE ... 151
- 11.1. Bars and Cocktail Lounges ... 151
- 11.2. Live Music and Performances ... 153
- 11.3. Nightclubs and Dance Venues ... 155
- 11.4. Cultural Events and Festivals ... 158
- 11.5. Evening Tours and Experiences ... 160
- Conclusion and Insider Tips for Visitors ... 164

SORRENTO TRAVEL PLANNER ... 167

MY EXPERIENCE IN SORRENTO

As I stepped off the train and onto the sun-drenched platform of Sorrento, I felt a wave of anticipation wash over me. Nestled on the cliffs of the Amalfi Coast, Sorrento is a place where the scent of lemons fills the air, and the azure sea stretches as far as the eye can see. I had heard tales of its beauty, but nothing could have prepared me for the breathtaking vistas that lay before me.

My first stroll through the town was like walking through a painting. The narrow, cobblestone streets, lined with vibrant shops and cafes, led me to Piazza Tasso, the heart of Sorrento. Here, the buzz of Vespas mingled with the chatter of locals and the laughter of tourists, creating a melody that is quintessentially Italian. I sipped on a limoncello, the local liqueur, and watched the world go by, feeling an overwhelming sense of contentment.

One of the highlights of my journey was a visit to the Cloister of San Francesco. This serene oasis, with its arched colonnades and lush gardens, provided a tranquil escape from the hustle and bustle of the town. As I wandered through the cloister, I couldn't help but feel a deep connection to the past, imagining the countless souls who had walked these same paths centuries ago. The culinary delights of Sorrento are something that will stay with me forever. From the freshest seafood to the most succulent pizzas, every meal was a celebration of flavors. Dining al fresco, with a view of the sun setting over the sea, was an experience that epitomized the essence of la dolce vita.

A boat trip to the nearby island of Capri was a dream come true. The journey across the turquoise waters, with the wind in my hair and the sun on my face, was exhilarating. Exploring the island's charming streets, taking in the stunning views from the Gardens of Augustus, and swimming in the crystal-clear waters of the Blue Grotto were moments of pure joy. One of the most magical experiences in Sorrento was watching the sunset from the cliffs. As the sky turned shades of pink and orange, and the sun dipped below the horizon, I felt a profound sense of peace. It was a reminder of the beauty and wonder that exists in the world, waiting to be discovered.

My time in Sorrento was more than just a journey; it was a journey of the soul. It taught me to appreciate the simple pleasures in life, to connect with the past, and to embrace the beauty of the present. Sorrento, with its timeless charm and breathtaking landscapes, is a place that captures the heart and inspires the spirit. As I boarded the train to leave, I couldn't help but feel a pang of sadness. Sorrento had become more than just a destination; it had become a part of me. But I knew that this was not a goodbye; it was simply an arrivederci. For I was certain that the allure of Sorrento would call me back again, to once more lose myself in its enchanting streets and be captivated by its stunning vistas.

To anyone considering a visit to this enchanting corner of the world, I say this: Sorrento is not just a place to see, but a place to feel. It is a destination that will touch your heart and leave an indelible mark on your soul. So pack your bags, open your heart, and get ready to fall in love with Sorrento, a gem on the Amalfi Coast that will steal your breath away and fill you with an insatiable desire to return.

SORRENTO FAQ?

1. What is the best time to visit Sorrento?
The best time to visit Sorrento is from April to June and September to October when the weather is pleasant, and the crowds are smaller. July and August are peak tourist months with higher temperatures and more crowds.

2. How do I get to Sorrento?
Sorrento is easily accessible by train, bus, or ferry. The nearest airport is Naples International Airport. From Naples, you can take the Circumvesuviana train or a bus to reach Sorrento. Ferries are also available from Naples and Capri.

3. Do I need a car in Sorrento?
A car is not necessary in Sorrento as the town is compact and walkable. Public transportation is available for exploring nearby attractions. However, if you plan to explore the Amalfi Coast extensively, a car might be convenient.

4. What are the must-visit attractions in Sorrento?
Must-visit attractions include the Marina Grande, Piazza Tasso, the Cloister of San Francesco, the Cathedral of Sorrento, and the Museo Correale. Don't miss taking a day trip to Capri, Pompeii, or the Amalfi Coast.

5. What is the currency in Sorrento?
The currency in Sorrento is the Euro (EUR). Credit cards are widely accepted, but it's advisable to carry some cash for smaller establishments.

6. What language is spoken in Sorrento?
Italian is the official language. However, English is widely spoken in tourist areas.

7. What are the best local dishes to try in Sorrento?

Try local specialties like gnocchi alla sorrentina, limoncello, seafood dishes, and delizia al limone (a lemon-flavored dessert).

8. Is Sorrento safe for tourists?

Sorrento is generally safe for tourists. However, like any tourist destination, it's advisable to take standard safety precautions and be aware of your surroundings.

9. What is the typical weather like in Sorrento?

Sorrento has a Mediterranean climate with mild, wet winters and warm, dry summers. Temperatures in summer can reach the high 20s°C (80s°F), while winter temperatures are usually in the low teens°C (50s°F).

10. Can I use my mobile phone in Sorrento?

Check with your mobile provider for international roaming options. Alternatively, you can purchase a local SIM card for data and calls.

11. Are there any beaches in Sorrento?

Sorrento has small beaches and bathing platforms, such as Marina Grande and Marina Piccola. For larger beaches, visit nearby towns like Positano or Amalfi.

12. What souvenirs should I bring back from Sorrento?

Popular souvenirs include limoncello, ceramics, inlaid woodwork, and handmade leather goods.

13. What is the typical dress code in Sorrento?

The dress code is casual but stylish. For dining out or visiting churches, it's advisable to dress modestly.

14. Are there any festivals or events in Sorrento?
Sorrento hosts various festivals and events throughout the year, including the Sorrento Film Festival, the Lemon Festival, and summer concerts in the Villa Comunale.

15. What are some good day trips from Sorrento?
Popular day trips include Capri, the Amalfi Coast, Pompeii, Herculaneum, and Mount Vesuvius.

Sorrento is a charming and vibrant destination with something for everyone. By knowing the answers to these frequently asked questions, you'll be well-prepared to make the most of your visit to this beautiful Italian town. Whether you're exploring its historic sites, savoring its culinary delights, or venturing out to nearby attractions, Sorrento is sure to leave a lasting impression on your heart.

WHY VISIT SORRENTO?

Sorrento stands as a testament to the beauty and charm of Italy. With its breathtaking vistas, rich history, and vibrant culture, this picturesque town beckons travelers from around the globe. In this session, we'll delve into the myriad reasons why Sorrento should be at the top of your travel bucket list.

Enchanting Natural Beauty

Sorrento's natural beauty is simply unparalleled. Perched atop cliffs that overlook the azure waters of the Tyrrhenian Sea, the town offers panoramic views that will leave you spellbound. The vibrant colors of the Mediterranean flora, the serene sunsets, and the gentle sea breeze create an atmosphere of tranquility and wonder. Whether you're strolling along the Marina Grande or gazing out from the Villa Comunale, Sorrento's picturesque landscapes are sure to captivate your heart.

Rich Historical Tapestry

Sorrento is steeped in history, with a tapestry that dates back to ancient times. The town's historic center, with its narrow alleys and charming piazzas, is a living museum that tells the stories of bygone eras. Landmarks such as the 14th-century Cloister of San Francesco and the Sedil Dominova offer glimpses into Sorrento's medieval past, while the ruins of the ancient Roman villa, Villa Pollio Felice, showcase its classical heritage. Exploring Sorrento is like taking a journey through time, where each corner holds a piece of the town's rich history.

Culinary Delights

Sorrento is a paradise for food lovers. The town is renowned for its delicious cuisine, which is a celebration of fresh, local ingredients. From the famous limoncello, made from the region's succulent lemons, to the mouthwatering seafood dishes, dining in Sorrento is an experience in itself. The town's trattorias and restaurants serve up traditional recipes passed down through generations, offering a taste of authentic Italian cooking that is both comforting and exquisite.

Vibrant Culture and Festivities

The cultural vibrancy of Sorrento is palpable. The town is alive with music, art, and festivals that showcase its rich traditions. The Sorrento Music Festival, held annually, fills the streets with the melodies of classical and contemporary music. Artisans can be seen crafting intricate inlaid woodwork, a centuries-old local art form. During the festive season, Sorrento transforms into a magical wonderland, with lights and decorations adorning the streets, making it a perfect destination to experience Italian celebrations.

Gateway to Wonders

Sorrento's strategic location makes it an ideal base for exploring the wonders of the Amalfi Coast and beyond. The enchanting islands of Capri and Ischia are just a short ferry ride away, offering their own unique landscapes and attractions. The historic sites of Pompeii and Herculaneum are within easy reach, providing a fascinating glimpse into the ancient Roman world. The stunning towns of Positano, Amalfi, and Ravello, with their cliffside villas and colorful architecture, are also easily accessible, making Sorrento the perfect starting point for an unforgettable Italian adventure.

Sorrento is a destination that captures the essence of Italy's beauty, history, and culture. Its enchanting landscapes, rich heritage, delectable cuisine, and vibrant festivities make it a place that appeals to all senses. Whether you're seeking relaxation, adventure, or cultural enrichment, Sorrento has something to offer. So, why visit Sorrento? Because it's not just a place to see; it's an experience to be lived, cherished, and remembered forever.

WHAT TO EXPECT FROM THIS GUIDE

Welcome to **"Sorrento Travel Guide 2024 And Beyond,"** your all-encompassing resource for exploring the enchanting town of Sorrento and its surrounding wonders. Located on the picturesque Amalfi Coast, Sorrento is a destination that promises an unforgettable journey filled with breathtaking landscapes, rich history, and vibrant culture. This guide is designed to provide you with all the essential information and insider tips to ensure a seamless and memorable experience in this Italian paradise.

Maps and Navigation

Our guide begins with detailed maps and navigation tools to help you orient yourself in Sorrento. You'll find user-friendly maps highlighting the main areas, attractions, and transportation routes, ensuring you can easily navigate the town's charming streets and picturesque surroundings. Whether you're exploring the historic center or venturing to nearby attractions, our navigation resources will keep you on the right path.

Accommodation Options

Sorrento offers a diverse range of accommodation options to suit every preference and budget. From luxurious hotels with stunning sea views to cozy bed and breakfasts nestled in the heart of the town, our guide provides an extensive overview of the best places to stay. We also cover charming boutique hotels, family-friendly resorts, and affordable vacation rentals, complete with recommendations and tips for choosing the perfect base for your Sorrentine adventure.

Transportation

Getting around Sorrento and the Amalfi Coast is an integral part of your travel experience. Our guide delves into the various transportation options available, including public buses, ferries, trains, and car rentals. We provide practical advice on navigating the local transport system, tips for scenic drives along the coast, and information on how to reach nearby destinations like Capri, Pompeii, and Naples.

Top Attractions

Discover the must-visit attractions that make Sorrento a captivating destination. Our guide highlights the town's iconic landmarks, such as the Marina Grande, Piazza Tasso, and the Cloister of San Francesco. We also explore the natural wonders of the region, including the breathtaking viewpoints, serene beaches, and hidden coves that await your exploration.

Practical Information and Travel Resources

To ensure a hassle-free journey, our guide covers all the practical information you'll need, from visa requirements and currency exchange to emergency contacts and health services. We also provide a list of useful websites, mobile apps, and travel resources to assist you in planning your trip and staying connected during your stay.

Culinary Delights

Sorrento is a haven for food enthusiasts, and our guide takes you on a culinary journey through the town's gastronomic delights. Learn about the local specialties, from succulent seafood dishes to the famous limoncello liqueur. We offer recommendations for the best restaurants, trattorias, and cafes where you can savor authentic Italian cuisine and experience the vibrant dining culture.

Culture and Heritage

Immerse yourself in Sorrento's rich culture and heritage with our comprehensive coverage of the town's history, art, and traditions. Explore ancient churches, museums, and galleries that showcase the artistic legacy of the region. Discover the local festivals and events that celebrate Sorrentine customs and offer a glimpse into the vibrant community life.

Outdoor Activities and Adventures

For those seeking adventure, Sorrento and its surroundings offer a plethora of outdoor activities. Our guide provides information on hiking trails, boat tours, water sports, and other exciting experiences that allow you to connect with the natural beauty of the

Amalfi Coast. Whether you're hiking the Path of the Gods or kayaking along the coastline, there's an adventure for every type of traveler.

Shopping

Sorrento is a shopper's paradise, and our guide highlights the best places to find unique souvenirs, local crafts, and high-quality products. From bustling markets to chic boutiques, we cover the top shopping spots where you can discover handmade ceramics, inlaid woodwork, and other treasures that reflect the town's artisanal traditions.

Day Trips and Excursions

Expand your horizons with our suggestions for day trips and excursions from Sorrento. Whether you're exploring the ancient ruins of Pompeii, visiting the glamorous island of Capri, or wandering through the picturesque towns of the Amalfi Coast, our guide ensures you make the most of your time in this captivating region.

Entertainment and Nightlife

Experience Sorrento's vibrant nightlife and entertainment scene with our curated recommendations. From lively bars and clubs to traditional music performances and cultural events, our guide helps you discover the best spots to enjoy the town's lively atmosphere after dark.

"Sorrento Comprehensive Guide 2024" is your key to unlocking the treasures of Sorrento and its enchanting surroundings. With this guide in hand, you're equipped with all the knowledge and tips you need to embark on an unforgettable journey. So pack your bags, embrace the spirit of adventure, and get ready to explore the captivating beauty of Sorrento, a destination that promises a lifetime of memories.

CHAPTER 1

INTRODUCTION TO SORRENTO

1.1. Overview of Sorrento

Perched on the cliffs overlooking the azure waters of the Tyrrhenian Sea, Sorrento is a town that epitomizes the beauty and allure of Italy's Amalfi Coast. With its picturesque landscapes, rich cultural heritage, and warm Mediterranean hospitality, Sorrento has captivated the hearts of travelers for centuries. In this overview, we delve into the essence of Sorrento, painting a vivid picture of what visitors can expect from this enchanting destination.

Enchanting Landscapes and Scenic Beauty

Sorrento is renowned for its breathtaking scenery, where rugged cliffs meet the sparkling sea, creating a panorama that is nothing short of spectacular. The town is adorned with lush gardens, fragrant lemon groves, and colorful buildings that cascade down the hillside, adding to its charm. Strolling along the Marina Grande, visitors can soak in the picturesque views of fishing boats bobbing in the harbor, while the sunset from the Villa Comunale offers an unforgettable spectacle, with the sky and sea merging in a kaleidoscope of colors.

A Rich Tapestry of History and Culture
Sorrento's history is as captivating as its landscapes. The town's origins date back to ancient times, and its strategic location has made it a crossroads of cultures throughout the centuries. Visitors can explore the narrow cobblestone streets of the historic center, where Romanesque churches, medieval buildings, and Renaissance palazzos tell the story of Sorrento's past. The Sedil Dominova and the Cloister of San Francesco are just a few of the architectural gems that reflect the town's rich cultural heritage.

Culinary Delights and Local Flavors
The culinary scene in Sorrento is a celebration of the region's bountiful produce and traditional recipes. The town is famous for its limoncello, a delightful lemon liqueur that captures the essence of Sorrento's sun-kissed lemons. Visitors can indulge in a variety of dishes that showcase the flavors of the Mediterranean, from fresh seafood and handmade pasta to delectable desserts like delizia al limone. Dining in Sorrento is not just about the food; it's an experience that combines the joy of eating with the pleasure of being in a beautiful setting.

Vibrant Lifestyle and Warm Hospitality
Sorrento's lifestyle is characterized by a relaxed Mediterranean pace, where the warmth of the sun is matched by the warmth of the locals. The town's piazzas are bustling with activity, offering a glimpse into the daily life of Sorrento. Piazza Tasso, the main square, is the perfect place to enjoy an espresso or aperitivo while watching the world go by. The hospitality of the Sorrentine people is legendary, and visitors are welcomed with open arms, making everyone feel like part of the community.

A Gateway to Adventure and Exploration

Sorrento serves as an ideal base for exploring the wonders of the Amalfi Coast and beyond. The town is well-connected by public transportation, making it easy to venture out to nearby attractions. The enchanting island of Capri, the ancient ruins of Pompeii and Herculaneum, and the stunning towns of Positano and Amalfi are all within reach. Whether it's hiking along the rugged coastline, taking a boat tour to hidden coves, or simply wandering through the lemon groves, Sorrento offers endless opportunities for adventure and exploration.

Sorrento is a town that captures the heart and soul of the Amalfi Coast. Its stunning landscapes, rich history, delicious cuisine, and friendly atmosphere make it a destination that offers something for every traveler. Whether you're seeking relaxation, adventure, or cultural immersion, Sorrento is a place that will leave you with memories to cherish for a lifetime. So come and experience the magic of Sorrento, where the beauty of Italy shines in all its splendor.

1.2. History and Significance

Sorrento is a town that whispers the tales of ancient civilizations, medieval conquests, and artistic renaissance. Its history is a mosaic of cultures and epochs, each leaving an indelible mark on the town's identity. In this detailed exploration, we delve into the historical significance of Sorrento, painting a vivid picture of its past for those who seek to journey through time.

The Ancient Roots of Sorrento

Sorrento's story begins in antiquity when it was known as Surrentum. The town's strategic location overlooking the Bay of Naples made it a prized possession for various civilizations. The Greeks first settled in Sorrento, drawn by its natural beauty and fertile lands. They were followed by the Romans, who turned Surrentum into a luxurious resort for the elite. Remnants of this opulent past can be seen in the ancient villas and the Baths of Queen Giovanna, where Roman nobility once bathed in the therapeutic waters.

Medieval Sorrento: A Tapestry of Conquest and Culture

The fall of the Roman Empire ushered in a new chapter for Sorrento. The town became a battleground for power, with Byzantines, Lombards, and Saracens vying for control. The medieval period was marked by fortifications, as seen in the remnants of the town walls and the imposing Sorrento Cathedral, which stands as a testament to the town's resilience during turbulent times. The Normans eventually brought stability to the region, and Sorrento flourished as a cultural and commercial hub.

Renaissance and Beyond: The Flourishing of Arts and Ideas

The Renaissance era breathed new life into Sorrento, with the town becoming a beacon of art and intellect. The Church of San Francesco, with its elegant cloister, became a center for religious and cultural gatherings. Sorrento's natural beauty inspired artists and writers, including the famous poet Torquato Tasso, who was born here. The town's artistic legacy continued through the centuries, with inlaid woodwork and ceramics becoming hallmarks of Sorrentine craftsmanship.

Sorrento in Modern Times: Preserving Heritage, Embracing Progress

The allure of Sorrento has stood the test of time, with the town evolving into a beloved tourist destination. The 19th and 20th centuries saw the arrival of illustrious visitors, from royalty to renowned artists, who were enchanted by Sorrento's charm. Today, the town strikes a balance between preserving its rich heritage and adapting to modernity. The historic center, with its ancient churches and palazzos, coexists with vibrant shops and cafes, offering a glimpse into Sorrento's past while embracing the present.

The history of Sorrento is a tapestry woven with threads of conquest, culture, and creativity. It is a town that has witnessed the rise and fall of empires, the blossoming of art, and the evolution of society. For visitors seeking to uncover the layers of Sorrento's past, the town offers a journey through time, where every stone and every view tells a story. In Sorrento, history is not just a relic of the past; it is a living, breathing presence that continues to shape the town's future.

1.3. Geography and Climate

Sorrento, a jewel nestled on the Amalfi Coast, is a harmonious blend of rugged cliffs, verdant hills, and azure waters. The town's geography and climate work in tandem to create a landscape that is as breathtaking as it is inviting. In this comprehensive exploration, we delve into the geographical wonders and climatic delights of Sorrento, providing visitors with all the information they need to fully appreciate the natural beauty of this enchanting destination.

The Geographical Tapestry of Sorrento

Perched on the Sorrentine Peninsula, Sorrento is a town where land meets sea in dramatic fashion. The peninsula itself is a geological marvel, extending into the Tyrrhenian Sea and forming the southern boundary of the Bay of Naples. Sorrento's cliffs, rising majestically from the sea, offer panoramic views of the surrounding waters and the distant peaks of Mount Vesuvius. The town is surrounded by a lush landscape, with olive groves, citrus orchards, and vineyards painting the countryside in vibrant hues. The fertile soil and mild climate make the region ideal for agriculture, and Sorrento is famed for its lemons, which are larger and sweeter than those found elsewhere.

The Climate of Sorrento: A Mediterranean Paradise

Sorrento enjoys a Mediterranean climate, characterized by mild, wet winters and warm, dry summers. This climate is a boon for both the natural environment and the visitors who flock to the town.

Winter: From December to February, temperatures in Sorrento average around 10°C (50°F). Rainfall is more frequent during these months, but the weather remains relatively mild compared to other European destinations. This makes Sorrento an attractive winter getaway for those seeking a respite from harsher climates.

Spring: March to May is a magical time in Sorrento as the town awakens from its winter slumber. The temperatures gradually rise, averaging between 15°C (59°F) and 20°C

(68°F). The countryside bursts into bloom, with lemon and orange groves fragrant with blossoms.

Summer: June to August marks the peak tourist season in Sorrento, with temperatures ranging from 25°C (77°F) to 30°C (86°F). The warm, sunny days are perfect for exploring the coast, lounging on the beach, or enjoying a cool drink in one of the town's many cafes.

Autumn: September to November sees a gentle cooling, with temperatures averaging between 20°C (68°F) and 25°C (77°F). The crowds begin to thin, making it an ideal time to explore the town and its surroundings in a more relaxed atmosphere.

The geography and climate of Sorrento are integral to its charm and appeal. The town's stunning cliffs, lush countryside, and sparkling sea create a setting that is both dramatic and serene. The mild Mediterranean climate ensures that Sorrento is a delightful destination year-round, offering visitors a chance to experience the natural beauty of the Amalfi Coast in all its seasonal variations. Whether basking in the summer sun or strolling through the fragrant groves in spring, Sorrento is a place where the wonders of nature are always on full display.

1.4. Local Customs and Traditions

Sorrento, a picturesque town on the Amalfi Coast, is not only renowned for its breathtaking landscapes but also for its rich tapestry of local customs and traditions. These cultural practices are the soul of Sorrento, offering visitors a glimpse into the town's vibrant heritage and community life. In this exploration, we delve into the customs and traditions that make Sorrento a captivating destination for those seeking an authentic cultural experience.

The Art of Hospitality

Hospitality is at the core of Sorrentine culture. The locals, known for their warmth and friendliness, welcome visitors with open arms, making everyone feel like part of the community. This tradition of hospitality is deeply rooted in the town's history, where the doors of Sorrento have always been open to travelers from around the world. Whether you're dining in a local trattoria or wandering through the narrow streets, the genuine smiles and greetings from the townsfolk embody the spirit of Sorrentine hospitality.

Celebrating Life with Festivals and Events

Sorrento's calendar is dotted with festivals and events that celebrate various aspects of its culture and history. One of the highlights is the Festa della Madonna del Carmine in July, where the town comes alive with processions, music, and fireworks in honor of the patron saint. The Sagra del Limone, or Lemon Festival, is another popular event that pays tribute to Sorrento's famous citrus fruit, with lemon-themed decorations, dishes, and drinks taking center stage.

The Culinary Traditions of Sorrento

Sorrento's culinary traditions are a reflection of its Mediterranean heritage, with an emphasis on fresh, locally-sourced ingredients. The town is famous for its lemons, which are used to make limoncello, a sweet and tangy liqueur that is a staple in Sorrentine homes. Seafood is also a key component of the local cuisine, with dishes like grilled octopus and spaghetti alle vongole (spaghetti with clams) being favorites among both locals and visitors. Dining in Sorrento is not just about the food; it's about sharing a meal with family and friends, celebrating the joy of togetherness.

The Craftsmanship of Sorrento

Sorrento is renowned for its exquisite craftsmanship, particularly in wood inlay and ceramics. The art of intarsia, or wood inlay, has been passed down through generations, with skilled artisans creating intricate designs on furniture, music boxes, and decorative objects. Similarly, the town's ceramic workshops produce beautiful hand-painted tiles, vases, and tableware that reflect the vibrant colors and patterns of the Mediterranean. These crafts are not only a source of pride for the locals but also cherished souvenirs for visitors.

A Connection to the Sea

The sea is an integral part of Sorrentine life, shaping the town's customs and traditions. Fishing has been a livelihood for many generations, and the daily catch is a central feature of Sorrento's cuisine. The Marina Grande, once the heart of the town's fishing industry, is now a charming harbor where locals and visitors alike gather to enjoy the sea breeze and the sound of the waves. The annual Regatta of the Ancient Maritime Republics, a historic boat race, celebrates Sorrento's maritime heritage and its connection to the sea. The local customs and traditions of Sorrento are a vibrant tapestry that weaves together the town's history, culture, and natural beauty. For visitors, experiencing these traditions firsthand is an opportunity to connect with the soul of Sorrento, to understand the values and practices that have shaped the community for centuries. Whether it's savoring a glass of limoncello, admiring the craftsmanship of a wood inlaid box, or joining in the festivities of a local festival, the traditions of Sorrento offer a rich and colorful journey into the heart of this enchanting Italian town.

1.5. Best Times to Visit

Sorrento, with its stunning vistas, rich cultural heritage, and Mediterranean charm, is a year-round destination that offers unique experiences in every season. However, the best time to visit Sorrento depends on your preferences for weather, crowd levels, and activities. In this comprehensive guide, we'll explore the nuances of each season, providing you with the information you need to plan your perfect Sorrentine getaway.

Spring: A Blooming Paradise

Spring, from March to May, is a delightful time to visit Sorrento. The weather is mild, with average temperatures ranging from 15°C (59°F) to 20°C (68°F), making it ideal for outdoor activities and sightseeing. The countryside is awash with color as flowers bloom and lemon groves become fragrant, creating a picturesque setting for your adventures. This season is also less crowded than summer, allowing you to explore Sorrento's beauty in a more relaxed atmosphere.

Summer: The Vibrant Peak Season

Summer, from June to August, is the peak tourist season in Sorrento. The weather is warm and sunny, with temperatures often reaching 30°C (86°F) or higher. This is the perfect time for beach lovers and water enthusiasts to enjoy the crystal-clear waters of the Tyrrhenian Sea. However, be prepared for larger crowds and higher prices, as this is the most popular time for visitors. Despite this, the lively atmosphere, with numerous festivals and events, adds to the allure of a summer visit.

Autumn: A Mellow Retreat

Autumn, from September to November, offers a mellow alternative to the bustling summer months. The temperatures remain pleasant, ranging from 20°C (68°F) to 25°C (77°F), and the crowds begin to thin out. This season is a great time to enjoy outdoor activities like hiking or exploring the Amalfi Coast without the summer heat. The autumn harvest brings a bounty of local produce to the markets, providing a culinary treat for food enthusiasts.

Winter: A Quiet Escape

Winter, from December to February, is the quietest season in Sorrento. The temperatures are cooler, averaging around 10°C (50°F), and there is a higher chance of rain. However, this is an excellent time to experience Sorrento's charm without the crowds. The town takes on a festive atmosphere during the Christmas season, with decorations and lights adding to its beauty. Additionally, winter is a great time to explore nearby cultural sites like Pompeii and Naples, as they are less crowded and more enjoyable to visit.

The best time to visit Sorrento ultimately depends on your preferences and what you want to experience. Spring and autumn offer a balance of pleasant weather and fewer crowds, making them ideal for those seeking a more relaxed visit. Summer is perfect for beach lovers and those who enjoy a vibrant atmosphere, while winter provides a tranquil escape and the opportunity to explore the region's cultural treasures.

Regardless of when you choose to visit, Sorrento's timeless beauty and welcoming spirit are sure to make your trip unforgettable.

CHAPTER 2

ACCOMMODATION OPTIONS

Click the link or Scan the QR Code with a device to view a comprehensive map of various Accommodation Options in Sorrento – https://shorturl.at/ltzGQ

2.1. Luxury Hotels and Resorts

Sorrento, a gem on the Amalfi Coast, is not only famed for its stunning landscapes and rich history but also for its exquisite luxury accommodations. These hotels and resorts offer an unparalleled experience, combining breathtaking views, exceptional service, and world-class amenities. In this detailed exploration, we delve into six of Sorrento's most luxurious hotels and resorts, providing you with all the information you need for an unforgettable stay in this enchanting town.

Grand Hotel Excelsior Vittoria

Perched atop the cliffs with panoramic views of the Bay of Naples, the Grand Hotel Excelsior Vittoria epitomizes luxury and elegance. Dating back to 1834, this iconic hotel boasts a rich history and has hosted numerous celebrities and royalty. The hotel features opulent rooms and suites, each uniquely decorated with antique furnishings and modern comforts. Guests can indulge in fine dining at the Michelin-starred Terrazza Bosquet, relax in the boutique spa, or wander through the lush private park. Prices for lodging start from around €500 per night, offering an unforgettable experience of timeless luxury.

Bellevue Syrene

The Bellevue Syrene, nestled on the cliffs overlooking the sea, offers a harmonious blend of historical charm and contemporary luxury. This 18th-century villa, once a private residence, has been transformed into a boutique hotel with elegantly designed rooms and suites that showcase stunning sea views. The hotel's Club Lounge offers complimentary snacks and drinks throughout the day, while the La Pergola Terrace is the perfect spot for a romantic dinner. With prices starting at approximately €400 per night, guests can enjoy a serene and luxurious retreat.

Hotel Parco dei Principi

Designed by the renowned architect Gio Ponti, Hotel Parco dei Principi is a masterpiece of modernist design set amidst a beautiful botanical garden. The hotel features a striking blue and white color scheme, with rooms offering breathtaking views of the sea or the lush gardens. Guests can relax by the stunning seawater pool, enjoy gourmet dining at the Gio Ponti restaurant, or take a short stroll to the private beach. Room rates begin at around €350 per night, providing a unique and stylish luxury experience.

Le Sirenuse

Le Sirenuse, a former 18th-century palazzo turned luxury hotel, exudes charm and sophistication. Located in the heart of Sorrento, the hotel offers enchanting views of the coastline from its elegantly furnished rooms and suites. The Michelin-starred La Sponda restaurant, illuminated by hundreds of candles, serves exquisite Mediterranean cuisine. Guests can unwind at the Aveda spa, sip cocktails at the chic Champagne Bar, or lounge by the beautiful pool. Prices for a stay at Le Sirenuse start from around €600 per night, offering an intimate and luxurious escape.

Villa Fiorentino

Villa Fiorentino is a luxurious boutique hotel that combines the intimacy of a private villa with the amenities of a world-class resort. Nestled in the hills above Sorrento, the hotel offers stunning views of the sea and the surrounding landscape. Each suite is uniquely designed, featuring contemporary decor and private terraces. Guests can enjoy the infinity pool, relax in the wellness center, or take part in cooking classes and wine tastings. With prices starting at approximately €450 per night, Villa Fiorentino provides a personalized and upscale experience.

Capo La Gala Hotel & Spa

Perched on a rocky cliff between Sorrento and Pompeii, Capo La Gala Hotel & Spa is a haven of luxury and tranquility. The hotel's nautical-themed rooms and suites are elegantly appointed, offering spectacular views of the Gulf of Naples. The Michelin-starred Maxi Restaurant serves innovative Mediterranean cuisine, while the Gouache Bar is perfect for sunset cocktails. The hotel's spa offers a range of treatments, and guests can relax by the seafront pool. Room rates begin at around €400 per night, making Capo La Gala an ideal choice for those seeking a luxurious coastal retreat. Sorrento's luxury hotels and resorts offer an array of choices for discerning travelers seeking an opulent and memorable stay. Whether you're drawn to the historical elegance of the Grand Hotel Excelsior Vittoria, the modernist charm of Hotel Parco dei Principi, or the intimate luxury of Villa Fiorentino, Sorrento has something to cater to every taste and preference. Each of these establishments provides not just a place to stay, but an experience that encapsulates the beauty, culture, and sophistication of this enchanting Italian town.

2.2. Mid-Range and Budget Hotels

Sorrento, a captivating town on the Amalfi Coast, is not only a haven for luxury travelers but also offers a range of mid-range and budget accommodations for those seeking comfort without the hefty price tag. These hotels provide an excellent base to explore Sorrento's enchanting beauty while offering amenities and services that ensure a comfortable stay. In this detailed exploration, we'll delve into six of Sorrento's mid-range and budget hotels, highlighting their features and offerings for travelers looking to experience the charm of Sorrento without breaking the bank.

Hotel La Badia

Nestled on a hillside overlooking the Bay of Naples, Hotel La Badia offers a tranquil retreat just a short walk from Sorrento's bustling center. This family-run hotel is set in a former monastery, blending historical charm with modern amenities. Guests can enjoy stunning sea views from the terrace, relax by the outdoor pool, or dine at the on-site restaurant serving local cuisine. Prices for lodging start from around €120 per night, making Hotel La Badia an excellent choice for those seeking a serene and affordable stay.

Palazzo Tasso

Located in the heart of Sorrento, Palazzo Tasso is a stylish boutique hotel that offers easy access to the town's attractions, shops, and restaurants. The hotel features contemporary rooms with vibrant decor, comfortable beds, and modern amenities. Guests can start their day with a complimentary breakfast served in the cozy breakfast room. With rates starting at approximately €100 per night, Palazzo Tasso is perfect for travelers looking for a chic and budget-friendly option in the center of Sorrento.

Hotel del Mare

Situated in the charming Marina Grande area, Hotel del Mare is a cozy hotel just steps away from the beach and a short walk from Sorrento's main square. The hotel offers comfortable rooms with nautical-themed decor, some with balconies offering sea views. Guests can enjoy a rooftop terrace with panoramic views, a lounge area, and a continental breakfast. Room rates begin at around €90 per night, providing a great value for those wanting to stay near the waterfront.

Casa Astarita Bed and Breakfast

Casa Astarita Bed and Breakfast is a charming accommodation option located on Corso Italia, Sorrento's main street. This family-run B&B is housed in a beautifully restored historic building and offers elegantly furnished rooms with modern comforts. Guests can enjoy a delicious breakfast with fresh local products each morning. With prices starting at about €80 per night, Casa Astarita is an excellent choice for travelers seeking a cozy and affordable stay in the heart of Sorrento.

Ulisse Deluxe Hostel

For budget-conscious travelers, Ulisse Deluxe Hostel offers a comfortable and affordable stay without compromising on amenities. Located a short walk from Sorrento's center, the hostel features a range of room options, from dormitories to private en-suite rooms. Guests can enjoy an indoor pool, a wellness center, and a buffet breakfast. Prices for lodging start from as low as €35 per night for a bed in a dormitory, making it an ideal choice for solo travelers and backpackers.

Il Roseto Resort

Il Roseto Resort is a charming bed and breakfast set in a lush garden filled with roses and lemon trees. Located just outside Sorrento's center, this family-run B&B offers a peaceful retreat with comfortable rooms and a swimming pool. Guests can enjoy a hearty breakfast with homemade cakes and local products. Room rates start from around €70 per night, providing a tranquil and budget-friendly option for those looking to escape the hustle and bustle of the town center.

Sorrento's mid-range and budget hotels offer a range of options for travelers seeking comfort and convenience without the high price tag. Whether you're looking for a tranquil retreat like Hotel La Badia, a stylish stay at Palazzo Tasso, or the budget-friendly Ulisse Deluxe Hostel, Sorrento has accommodations to suit every preference and budget. These hotels provide an excellent base to explore the stunning landscapes, rich history, and vibrant culture of this enchanting Italian town.

2.3. Bed and Breakfasts and Guesthouses

Sorrento, a picturesque town on the Amalfi Coast, is not only known for its stunning landscapes and rich history but also for its warm hospitality. Bed and breakfasts and guesthouses in Sorrento offer a more intimate and personalized lodging experience, allowing visitors to immerse themselves in the local culture. In this detailed exploration, we'll delve into six of Sorrento's delightful bed and breakfasts and guesthouses, highlighting their unique features and offerings for travelers seeking a cozy and authentic stay.

Maison Tofani

Maison Tofani is a charming bed and breakfast located in the heart of Sorrento's historic center. Housed in an 18th-century building, it boasts elegantly furnished rooms with frescoed ceilings and modern amenities. Guests can enjoy a sumptuous breakfast served in a beautiful dining room or on the rooftop terrace with panoramic views. Prices for lodging start from around €150 per night, making Maison Tofani an exquisite choice for those seeking a blend of history and luxury.

Magi House Relais

Nestled in a quiet alley just steps away from Sorrento's main square, Piazza Tasso, Magi House Relais offers stylish and contemporary accommodations. The guesthouse features a range of room options, from cozy double rooms to spacious suites with kitchenettes. Guests can take advantage of the rooftop terrace for relaxation and sunbathing. Room rates begin at approximately €120 per night, providing a chic and comfortable stay in the heart of Sorrento.

Casa Dominova

Casa Dominova is a quaint bed and breakfast situated in the historic center of Sorrento, near the charming Sedil Dominova building. This family-run B&B offers cozy rooms with traditional decor and modern comforts. Guests can enjoy a delightful breakfast in the peaceful garden courtyard, surrounded by lemon trees. Prices for lodging start from around €80 per night, making Casa Dominova a charming and affordable option for travelers.

Villa La Contessina

Located near the beautiful Marina Grande, Villa La Contessina offers an elegant and serene retreat in Sorrento. This luxurious guesthouse features spacious and beautifully decorated suites, each with a private terrace or garden. Guests can enjoy a lush Mediterranean garden, a solarium, and a personalized concierge service. Room rates start from around €200 per night, providing an upscale and tranquil experience.

Palazzo Montefusco

Palazzo Montefusco is a boutique bed and breakfast located in the heart of Sorrento's shopping district. It offers modern and stylish accommodations with a focus on comfort and design. Guests can indulge in a gourmet breakfast with homemade pastries and local specialties. The B&B also provides a cozy lounge area and personalized service. Prices for lodging begin at approximately €130 per night, making Palazzo Montefusco a fashionable choice for discerning travelers.

Relais Correale Rooms & Garden

Set in a 19th-century villa surrounded by a lush citrus grove, Relais Correale Rooms & Garden offers a peaceful escape just a short walk from Sorrento's center. The guesthouse features elegantly furnished rooms with garden views and a relaxing outdoor area. Guests can enjoy a delicious breakfast served in the garden or the charming breakfast room. Room rates start from around €100 per night, offering a serene and picturesque stay in Sorrento. Sorrento's bed and breakfasts and guesthouses provide a wonderful opportunity for travelers to experience the town's hospitality in a more intimate setting. Whether you're looking for the historical charm of Maison Tofani, the contemporary style of Magi House Relais, or the serene ambiance of Relais Correale Rooms & Garden, Sorrento offers a variety of cozy accommodations to suit your preferences. These establishments not only provide a comfortable place to stay but also offer a glimpse into the local culture and lifestyle, making your visit to Sorrento truly memorable.

2.4. Self-Catering Apartments and Villas

Sorrento, a jewel on the Amalfi Coast, offers not only stunning views and rich history but also a variety of self-catering apartments and villas for those seeking a more independent and flexible travel experience. These accommodations provide the comfort of home with the added luxury of privacy and space, allowing visitors to immerse themselves in the local lifestyle. In this detailed exploration, we'll delve into six of Sorrento's finest self-catering apartments and villas, highlighting their features and offerings for travelers looking for a personalized stay.

Villa Eliana

Perched on the hills overlooking the Bay of Naples, Villa Eliana is a luxurious retreat that offers breathtaking panoramic views. This modern villa features spacious living areas, elegantly furnished bedrooms, a fully equipped kitchen, and expansive terraces for outdoor dining and relaxation. Guests can enjoy the infinity pool surrounded by lush gardens. Prices for lodging start from around €500 per night, making Villa Eliana an ideal choice for those seeking exclusivity and serenity.

Sorrento Flats

Located in the heart of Sorrento, Sorrento Flats offers a range of stylish apartments and studios that combine modern amenities with traditional Italian charm. Each unit is uniquely decorated and equipped with a kitchenette, providing the perfect base for exploring the town and its surroundings. Guests can take advantage of the communal rooftop terrace with stunning views of the historical center. Room rates begin at approximately €120 per night, offering a chic and convenient stay in the heart of Sorrento.

Casa Sorrentina

Casa Sorrentina is a collection of charming self-catering apartments situated near Piazza Tasso, Sorrento's main square. These apartments feature a blend of classic and contemporary decor, with fully equipped kitchens, comfortable living spaces, and private balconies. Guests can enjoy the convenience of being close to shops, restaurants, and attractions. Prices for lodging start from around €100 per night, providing a cozy and central home away from home.

Villa La Terrazza

Villa La Terrazza is a historic villa set on the cliffs of Sorrento, offering stunning views of the sea and Mount Vesuvius. The villa features a selection of elegant apartments, each with a private terrace, fully equipped kitchen, and spacious living areas. Guests can relax in the beautiful Mediterranean garden or take a dip in the infinity pool. Room rates start from around €200 per night, making Villa La Terrazza a luxurious and scenic choice for a self-catering stay.

La Piazzetta Guest House

La Piazzetta Guest House provides a range of modern apartments in the heart of Sorrento, just steps away from the vibrant Piazza Tasso. Each apartment is equipped with a kitchenette, comfortable furnishings, and contemporary amenities. Guests can enjoy the convenience of self-catering while being close to all the action. Prices for lodging begin at approximately €90 per night, offering an affordable and stylish option for independent travelers.

Casa Azzurra

Casa Azzurra is a delightful self-catering villa located in a quiet residential area of Sorrento. This spacious villa features a fully equipped kitchen, comfortable living areas, and a lovely garden with an outdoor dining area. Guests can enjoy a peaceful retreat while being just a short drive from the town center and the beautiful Amalfi Coast. Room rates start from around €150 per night, providing a tranquil and comfortable base for exploring Sorrento and its surroundings. Sorrento's self-catering apartments and villas offer travelers the freedom to experience the town at their own pace. Whether you're looking for the luxury of Villa Eliana, the convenience of Sorrento Flats, or the tranquility of Casa Azzurra, these accommodations provide the perfect blend of comfort, privacy, and flexibility. With the added benefits of fully equipped kitchens and spacious living areas, guests can enjoy the comforts of home while soaking up the beauty and charm of Sorrento.

2.5. Hostels and Affordable Accommodations

Sorrento, a captivating town on the Amalfi Coast, is not only a destination for luxury travelers but also offers a variety of hostels and affordable accommodations for budget-conscious visitors. These establishments provide a comfortable and sociable environment, allowing travelers to explore Sorrento's beauty without breaking the bank. In this detailed exploration, we'll delve into six of Sorrento's best hostels and affordable accommodations, highlighting their features and offerings for travelers seeking value and convenience.

Hostel Sorrento

Hostel Sorrento is a popular choice for backpackers and budget travelers, located just a short walk from the town center and the train station. This hostel offers dormitory rooms with shared facilities, as well as private rooms with en-suite bathrooms. Guests can enjoy a communal kitchen, a lounge area, and a terrace with views of the surrounding hills. Prices for lodging start from around €25 per night for a bed in a dormitory, making Hostel Sorrento an excellent option for those seeking a social and affordable stay.

Seven Hostel

Seven Hostel, situated in the nearby town of Sant'Agnello, is a stylish and modern hostel that offers a range of accommodations, from shared dormitories to private rooms. The hostel features a rooftop terrace with panoramic views of the Bay of Naples, a bar, and a restaurant serving local cuisine. Guests can also take advantage of the hostel's organized tours and activities. Room rates begin at approximately €20 per night for a bed in a dormitory, providing a chic and budget-friendly choice for travelers.

Florida Hostel & Hotel

Located in a quiet area of Sorrento, Florida Hostel & Hotel offers a blend of hostel-style dormitories and hotel rooms, catering to a variety of budgets. The property boasts a swimming pool, a garden, and a bar, creating a relaxing atmosphere for guests. The hostel also provides a continental breakfast and has a communal kitchen for self-catering. Prices for lodging start from around €30 per night for a bed in a dormitory, making it a great value for those looking for affordable comfort.

Ulisse Deluxe Hostel

Ulisse Deluxe Hostel is a budget-friendly accommodation that offers the amenities of a hotel at hostel prices. Located in the heart of Sorrento, the hostel provides a range of room options, including dormitories, private rooms, and family suites. Guests can enjoy an indoor pool, a wellness center, and a buffet breakfast. Room rates start from around €35 per night for a bed in a dormitory, offering a comfortable and economical stay in central Sorrento.

Casa del Monacone

Casa del Monacone is a unique and affordable guesthouse located in a former monastery, just a short distance from Sorrento's main attractions. The guesthouse offers simple but comfortable rooms with shared bathrooms, a communal kitchen, and a peaceful courtyard. Guests can experience a tranquil and authentic stay, with prices starting at approximately €50 per night for a private room.

Ostello delle Sirene

Ostello delle Sirene is a budget-friendly hostel situated in the heart of Sorrento, close to the train station and the main square. The hostel offers dormitory rooms with shared facilities, as well as private rooms with en-suite bathrooms. Guests can make use of the communal kitchen, lounge area, and free Wi-Fi. Prices for lodging begin at around €25 per night for a bed in a dormitory, making Ostello delle Sirene an ideal choice for budget-conscious travelers seeking convenience and comfort.

Sorrento's hostels and affordable accommodations provide budget-friendly options for travelers looking to experience the charm of this Amalfi Coast town without spending a fortune. Whether you prefer the social atmosphere of Hostel Sorrento, the stylish ambiance of Seven Hostel, or the tranquility of Casa del Monacone, there is a range of options to suit your preferences and budget. These establishments not only offer a place to rest but also the opportunity to meet fellow travelers and make lasting memories in the beautiful setting of Sorrento.

CHAPTER 3

TRANSPORTATION IN SORRENTO

3.1. Getting to Sorrento: Air, Train, and Road Options

Nestled along the stunning Amalfi Coast of Italy, Sorrento beckons travelers with its picturesque landscapes, rich history, and vibrant culture. Whether you're drawn to its charming streets, breathtaking views of the Mediterranean Sea, or the tantalizing aroma of lemon groves, Sorrento promises an unforgettable experience. To embark on this journey, understanding the various transportation options available is crucial.

By Air: For visitors arriving from distant destinations, air travel offers convenience and efficiency. Naples International Airport (NAP), also known as Capodichino Airport, serves as the primary gateway to Sorrento. Several major airlines operate flights to

Naples from various international and domestic locations. Airlines such as Alitalia, Lufthansa (https://www.lufthansa.com/), British Airways (https://www.britishairways.com/), and EasyJet offer direct or connecting flights to Naples from major cities worldwide.

Upon arrival at Naples Airport, travelers can opt for various modes of transportation to reach Sorrento. The most popular choice is the shuttle bus service, which provides a direct and comfortable journey to Sorrento's city center at a cost of approximately €10-€15 per person. Alternatively, taxis are readily available outside the airport terminals, albeit at a higher cost of around €90-€120. For those seeking a more adventurous route, renting a car offers the flexibility to explore the scenic coastal roads at their own pace, with rental prices starting from €30-€50 per day.

By Train:

Train travel presents another convenient option for reaching Sorrento, especially for those already within Italy or neighboring countries. The Circumvesuviana railway network connects Naples to Sorrento, offering regular and affordable services throughout the day. Travelers arriving at Naples Central Station can easily transfer to the Circumvesuviana line, located within the same station complex.

The journey from Naples to Sorrento via train showcases breathtaking views of Mount Vesuvius and the Bay of Naples, adding to the allure of the travel experience. It's essential to note the timetable and ensure catching the correct train, as the Circumvesuviana line serves multiple destinations along the route. Train tickets typically cost around €4-€6 per person for a one-way journey.

By Road:

Road travel provides an opportunity to savor the scenic beauty of the Amalfi Coast en route to Sorrento. Visitors driving from Naples or other nearby cities can follow the A3 motorway towards Salerno, then continue along the breathtaking SS145 coastal road towards Sorrento. While this route offers stunning vistas of the coastline, it's important to be prepared for narrow and winding roads, especially during peak tourist seasons.

For those preferring a more relaxed journey, private car services and shuttle buses are available for hire, offering door-to-door transportation from Naples or other nearby cities directly to Sorrento. Additionally, rental car options abound at Naples Airport and in the surrounding areas, providing flexibility for independent exploration. Rental car prices typically start from €40-€60 per day, depending on the vehicle type and rental duration. You can find rental car options and make bookings through websites such as Rentalcars.com or AutoEurope.com.

Reaching Sorrento is a seamless endeavor with multiple transportation options catering to diverse preferences and budgets. Whether arriving by air, train, or road, visitors are greeted with the promise of unparalleled beauty and enchantment awaiting them in this idyllic coastal town. With careful planning and a sense of adventure, embarking on the journey to Sorrento is the first step towards creating cherished memories that will last a lifetime.

3.2. Public Transportation: Buses and Taxis

Navigating Sorrento's picturesque streets and exploring its surrounding attractions is made convenient through its well-established public transportation system. Whether you're seeking to meander through the town's historic center or venture further along the Amalfi Coast, buses and taxis offer accessible and efficient means of travel. Understanding the various options available, their prices, and how to navigate effectively ensures a seamless and enjoyable experience for visitors.

Buses in Sorrento:

Sorrento boasts a comprehensive network of buses operated by companies such as the Circumvesuviana and SITA. These buses serve both local routes within Sorrento and destinations further afield, including nearby towns along the Amalfi Coast and the archaeological sites of Pompeii and Herculaneum. Visitors can purchase tickets directly from ticket booths at major bus terminals or from authorized vendors such as tobacco shops and newsstands. It's important to note that tickets are typically sold as single rides or as day passes, providing unlimited travel within a specified timeframe.

The cost of bus tickets varies depending on the distance traveled and the type of service. For short journeys within Sorrento, a single ride ticket may cost around €1.50-€2.00, while day passes offering unlimited travel within Sorrento and neighboring areas may range from €5.00-€10.00 per person. Timetables and route maps are readily available at bus stops and tourist information centers, allowing visitors to plan their journeys effectively. Additionally, smartphone apps such as Moovit and Google Maps provide real-time information on bus routes, schedules, and estimated arrival times, enhancing the convenience of using public transportation in Sorrento.

Taxis in Sorrento:

For those seeking a more direct and personalized mode of transportation, taxis offer a convenient alternative in Sorrento. Taxis are readily available throughout the town, particularly in busy areas such as Piazza Tasso and the train station. Visitors can hail taxis on the street or request one through taxi stands located at designated points around Sorrento.

Taxi fares in Sorrento are regulated by a tariff system, with rates determined by factors such as distance traveled and time of day. As a general guideline, expect initial fares to start at around €5.00-€6.00, with additional charges applied for each kilometer traveled. It's advisable to confirm the fare with the driver before beginning your journey, particularly for longer trips or those involving special requests such as luggage transport or late-night travel.

Navigating Public Transportation Effectively:

To navigate Sorrento's public transportation system effectively, visitors are encouraged to familiarize themselves with route maps, timetables, and fare structures. Planning ahead and allowing sufficient time for travel ensures a stress-free experience while exploring the town and its surrounding areas. Utilizing smartphone apps and online resources for real-time information can also enhance the efficiency of using buses and taxis in Sorrento.

Moreover, seeking assistance from local residents or staff at hotels and tourist information centers can provide valuable insights and recommendations for navigating public transportation. Many locals are happy to offer guidance and assistance to visitors, further enhancing the overall travel experience in Sorrento.

In conclusion, buses and taxis serve as indispensable modes of public transportation in Sorrento, offering visitors convenient and accessible options for exploring the town and its surrounding attractions. By understanding the various services available, their prices, and how to navigate effectively, visitors can maximize their time and enjoyment while immersing themselves in the beauty and charm of Sorrento and the Amalfi Coast.

3.3. Walking and Scooter Rentals

Exploring Sorrento on foot or by scooter offers visitors the opportunity to immerse themselves fully in the town's vibrant atmosphere, charming streets, and stunning coastal views. With pedestrian-friendly pathways and scenic routes, walking and scooter rentals provide convenient and flexible options for navigating Sorrento and its surrounding areas. Understanding the various rental options available, their prices, and how to navigate effectively ensures a memorable and enjoyable experience for visitors.

Walking in Sorrento:

Sorrento's compact size and pedestrian-friendly layout make it ideal for exploring on foot. Visitors can stroll along the town's cobblestone streets, lined with quaint shops, cafes, and historic landmarks. Popular walking routes include the Corso Italia, a bustling thoroughfare brimming with boutiques and gelaterias, and the Via San Cesareo, known for its vibrant atmosphere and lively street performers.

For those seeking a more leisurely pace, the clifftop pathways overlooking the Bay of Naples offer breathtaking panoramic views of the sea and coastline. Visitors can also venture beyond the town center to explore hidden gems such as the Villa Comunale park, with its lush gardens and scenic overlooks.

Scooter Rentals in Sorrento:

Scooter rentals provide an exciting and convenient way to explore Sorrento and its surrounding areas with greater speed and flexibility. Several rental companies in Sorrento offer a range of scooter options to suit different preferences and skill levels. One reputable rental company is Scooter Rental Sorrento, located at Via degli Aranci 25. Their website, Scooter Rental Sorrento, provides detailed information on available scooter models, rental rates, and booking options.

Another popular option is Sorrento Scooter Rental, situated at Via degli Aranci 77. Sorrento Scooter Rental offers online reservations and provides information on safety guidelines, insurance coverage, and scooter accessories. Rental prices for scooters typically range from €30-€50 per day, with discounts available for longer rental periods.

Navigating Walking and Scooter Rentals Effectively:

To navigate Sorrento effectively with walking or scooter rentals, visitors should first familiarize themselves with the town's layout and main points of interest. Maps and guidebooks are valuable resources for planning walking routes and identifying scooter-friendly areas. Additionally, considering factors such as terrain, traffic conditions, and local regulations ensures a safe and enjoyable experience while exploring Sorrento.

When renting scooters, it's important to choose a reputable rental company that provides well-maintained vehicles and comprehensive insurance coverage. Prior to embarking on a scooter excursion, visitors should acquaint themselves with basic scooter operation and safety practices, including wearing helmets and adhering to traffic laws. For walking tours, joining guided walking tours or hiring local guides can enhance the experience by providing historical and cultural insights into Sorrento's landmarks and attractions. Many tour operators offer themed walking tours focusing on specific aspects of Sorrento's history, cuisine, or architecture.

Walking and scooter rentals offer visitors convenient and flexible options for exploring Sorrento and its surrounding areas. By understanding the various rental options available, their prices, and how to navigate effectively, visitors can maximize their time and enjoyment while immersing themselves in the beauty and charm of Sorrento and the Amalfi Coast.

3.4. Ferries and Boat Transfers

Ferries and boat transfers offer visitors a scenic and convenient means of exploring Sorrento's coastal beauty and accessing nearby destinations such as Capri, Amalfi, and Positano. With their frequent departures and stunning views of the Mediterranean Sea, these waterborne modes of transportation provide an unforgettable experience for travelers. Understanding the various ferry and boat transfer options available, their prices, and how to navigate effectively ensures a seamless and enjoyable journey for visitors.

Ferries to Capri:

One of the most popular ferry routes from Sorrento is to the enchanting island of Capri. Several ferry companies operate regular services between Sorrento and Capri, including Caremar, NLG, and SNAV. Ferries depart from Sorrento's Marina Piccola port, located near the town center, offering convenient access for visitors.

Caremar, one of the leading ferry operators, provides daily departures to Capri, with multiple sailings throughout the day. Visitors can purchase tickets directly at the ticket offices located at Marina Piccola or book in advance through Caremar's official website, Caremar. Ticket prices for the Sorrento-Capri route typically range from €20-€30 per person for a one-way journey, with discounts available for round-trip tickets.

NLG (Navigazione Libera del Golfo) and SNAV also offer ferry services to Capri from Sorrento, with similar schedules and ticket prices. NLG's website, https://www.nlg.it/en/, provides information on schedules, ticket prices, and booking options. Likewise, SNAV's website, https://www.snav.it/en/, offers online reservations and details on their ferry services to Capri.

Boat Transfers to Amalfi and Positano:

For travelers wishing to explore the charming towns of the Amalfi Coast, boat transfers offer a scenic and efficient mode of transportation from Sorrento. Several companies provide boat transfer services to destinations such as Amalfi and Positano, including Positano Jet and Travelmar.

Positano Jet operates daily boat transfers from Sorrento to Positano, departing from Marina Piccola. Their website, https://www.traghettilines.it/, offers online reservations and information on schedules, ticket prices, and departure points. Travelmar also offers boat transfers to Positano and other Amalfi Coast destinations, with ticket prices typically ranging from €25-€35 per person for a one-way journey.

Navigating effectively with ferries and boat transfers in Sorrento involves planning ahead and checking schedules, ticket prices, and departure points in advance. Visitors should arrive at the port early to purchase tickets and ensure timely boarding. Additionally, considering factors such as weather conditions and sea swell is important, as boat services may be affected during inclement weather.

Ferries and boat transfers offer visitors a memorable and scenic way to explore Sorrento and its surrounding coastal destinations. By understanding the various ferry and boat transfer options available, their prices, and how to navigate effectively, travelers can enjoy a seamless and unforgettable journey while immersing themselves in the beauty and charm of the Amalfi Coast.

3.5. Accessibility for Disabled Travelers

Exploring Sorrento's enchanting streets, picturesque coastline, and historic landmarks should be an experience accessible to all travelers, including those with disabilities. While Sorrento, like many European destinations, may present challenges for disabled travelers, efforts have been made to improve accessibility and accommodate diverse needs. From transportation options to accommodation and attractions, here's a comprehensive guide to navigating Sorrento for disabled travelers:

Transportation:

Sorrento's public transportation system includes buses and trains, but accessibility can vary. Most buses in Sorrento are equipped with ramps or lifts for wheelchair access, although some may have limited space for mobility devices. It's advisable to inquire about accessibility when boarding the bus and to allow extra time for boarding and disembarking. The Circumvesuviana train line, connecting Sorrento to Naples and other nearby towns, generally offers limited accessibility for wheelchair users due to stairs at station entrances and narrow aisles inside the trains. For disabled travelers seeking more accessible transportation options, private car services or wheelchair-accessible taxis may be preferable. Several taxi companies in Sorrento offer vehicles equipped with ramps or lifts for wheelchair access, although it's recommended to book in advance to ensure availability.

Accommodation:

When choosing accommodation in Sorrento, disabled travelers should prioritize hotels and guesthouses with accessible facilities. Many hotels in Sorrento offer accessible rooms equipped with features such as widened doorways, grab bars in bathrooms, and roll-in showers. It's advisable to contact hotels directly to inquire about specific accessibility features and to confirm availability during the booking process. Additionally, online booking platforms often provide filters for searching specifically for accessible accommodations.

Attractions and Sightseeing:

While Sorrento's charming streets and scenic viewpoints are accessible to all, some historic sites and attractions may pose challenges for disabled travelers due to architectural barriers. However, efforts have been made to improve accessibility at popular tourist sites. For example, some archaeological sites, such as Pompeii and Herculaneum, offer designated accessible routes and facilities for disabled visitors. When planning sightseeing activities, it's recommended to research accessibility information for specific attractions in advance. Many tourist attractions in Sorrento provide details on accessibility features, such as wheelchair ramps, elevators, and accessible restrooms, on their official websites or through visitor information services.

Beach Access:

Sorrento's stunning coastline boasts several beaches, but accessibility for disabled travelers may vary. While some beaches offer accessible facilities, such as wheelchair ramps and accessible restrooms, others may have limited accessibility due to stairs or uneven terrain. It's advisable to research accessible beach options in Sorrento and inquire about accessibility features before planning a visit.

Navigating Streets and Sidewalks:

Sorrento's narrow cobblestone streets and uneven sidewalks can pose challenges for disabled travelers, particularly those using mobility devices. However, efforts have been made to improve accessibility in the town center, with some areas featuring smoother pavement and curb ramps. When navigating streets and sidewalks, disabled travelers should exercise caution and plan routes carefully to avoid steep inclines or obstacles. While Sorrento may present challenges for disabled travelers, efforts have been made to improve accessibility and accommodate diverse needs. By researching accessibility information in advance, prioritizing accessible transportation and accommodation options, and planning sightseeing activities carefully, disabled travelers can enjoy a memorable and fulfilling experience exploring the beauty and charm of Sorrento.

CHAPTER 4

TOP ATTRACTIONS

Click the link or Scan the QR Code with a device to view a comprehensive map of Top Attractions in Sorrento – https://shorturl.at/ACHT6

4.1. Sorrento Historic Center and Piazza Tasso

Sorrento stands as a timeless testament to the region's rich history, culture, and beauty. Among its many treasures, the Sorrento Historic Center and Piazza Tasso emerge as vibrant hubs that beckon travelers from around the world. Stepping into this enchanting district is like stepping into a living canvas, where history, tradition, and modernity blend seamlessly to create an unforgettable experience.

Location and Accessibility:

The Sorrento Historic Center and Piazza Tasso are situated in the heart of Sorrento, a picturesque town overlooking the Bay of Naples. Easily accessible by various means of transportation, Sorrento is approximately a 1-hour drive from Naples International Airport and can also be reached by train from major Italian cities such as Naples and Rome. Once in Sorrento, the Historic Center and Piazza Tasso are conveniently located within walking distance from the town's central train station and bus terminal.

Entry Fee and Hours of Operation:

One of the most appealing aspects of visiting the Sorrento Historic Center and Piazza Tasso is that there is no entry fee. The area is open to visitors year-round, allowing travelers to immerse themselves in its charm at any time of day or season.

Why Visit?

From its winding cobblestone streets to its bustling squares, the Sorrento Historic Center exudes an irresistible charm that captivates all who wander its paths. Here are just a few reasons why a visit to this enchanting district is an absolute must:

Historical Significance:

The Sorrento Historic Center is steeped in history, with its origins dating back to ancient times. As you meander through its labyrinthine streets, you'll encounter a fascinating tapestry of architectural styles spanning centuries, from Roman ruins and medieval churches to elegant Renaissance palaces. Each corner holds a story waiting to be discovered, offering visitors a glimpse into Sorrento's rich and storied past.

Cultural Delights:

Piazza Tasso serves as the vibrant heart of Sorrento's Historic Center, pulsating with energy and activity day and night. Named after the renowned Italian poet Torquato Tasso, the square is lined with charming cafes, restaurants, and shops, where visitors can indulge in the flavors of the region and browse local artisanal crafts. Whether sipping on a freshly brewed espresso or sampling traditional limoncello liqueur, Piazza Tasso offers a sensory journey through the essence of Italian culture.

Scenic Beauty:

Surrounded by soaring cliffs and azure waters, Sorrento boasts some of the most breathtaking vistas in Italy. From Piazza Tasso, visitors can marvel at panoramic views of the Bay of Naples and the majestic Mount Vesuvius in the distance. As the sun sets over the horizon, casting a golden glow upon the landscape, the scene becomes nothing short of magical, inviting travelers to pause and soak in the beauty that surrounds them.

Authentic Atmosphere:

What truly sets the Sorrento Historic Center apart is its authentic atmosphere, where old-world charm meets modern sophistication. Unlike some tourist destinations that feel overly commercialized, Sorrento exudes a genuine sense of hospitality and warmth, inviting visitors to experience la dolce vita in its purest form. Whether chatting with locals in the town square or strolling through its hidden alleyways, you'll feel welcomed like a member of the Sorrentine community.

Practical Information:

- While there is no entry fee to explore the Sorrento Historic Center and Piazza Tasso, it's a good idea to bring comfortable walking shoes, as the terrain can be uneven.
- For those traveling by car, parking may be limited in the town center, so it's advisable to use public transportation whenever possible.
- To fully immerse yourself in the local culture, consider timing your visit to coincide with one of Sorrento's many festivals or events, such as the Feast of St. Anthony or the Sorrento Music Festival.
- Don't forget to sample the local cuisine, including fresh seafood dishes, homemade pasta, and, of course, the famous Sorrentine lemons, which are used to make the region's signature limoncello liqueur.

Sorrento's Historic Center and Piazza Tasso stand as quintessential must-see attractions that capture the essence of Italian culture, history, and hospitality. Whether you're drawn to its captivating architecture, vibrant atmosphere, or culinary delights, a visit to Sorrento's Historic Center promises an unforgettable journey filled with warmth, beauty, and boundless charm. So, pack your bags, embark on an adventure, and let Sorrento weave its magic around you.

4.2. Marina Grande and Fishing Harbor

Nestled along the stunning coastline of Sorrento in Southern Italy, Marina Grande and the Fishing Harbor emerge as quintessential Mediterranean destinations that beckon travelers seeking to immerse themselves in the region's rich maritime heritage and natural beauty. These picturesque waterfront locales offer a glimpse into Sorrento's past while providing a vibrant backdrop for unforgettable experiences.

Location and Accessibility:

Marina Grande and the Fishing Harbor are conveniently situated just a short stroll from Sorrento's bustling town center. Visitors can easily reach these enchanting destinations on foot, following the scenic coastal promenade that winds its way along the shoreline. For those arriving by car, ample parking is available nearby, while public transportation options such as buses and taxis provide additional convenience.

Entry Fee and Hours of Operation:

Entrance to Marina Grande and the Fishing Harbor is free of charge, allowing visitors to explore at their leisure. The areas are accessible year-round, although opening hours for waterfront cafes, restaurants, and shops may vary depending on the season.

Why Visit?

Marina Grande and the Fishing Harbor offer a unique blend of natural beauty, historical significance, and authentic charm that make them must-see attractions for visitors to Sorrento. Here are just a few reasons why a visit to these coastal gems is an essential part of any Sorrentine experience:

Historical and Cultural Significance:

Marina Grande has long been the beating heart of Sorrento's maritime traditions, serving as a fishing village since ancient times. Its colorful waterfront buildings and bustling harbor evoke a sense of nostalgia for a bygone era when fishing was the lifeblood of the community. Visitors can wander the narrow streets lined with traditional fishermen's cottages, immersing themselves in the sights, sounds, and scents of Sorrento's seafaring heritage.

Scenic Beauty:

The azure waters of the Mediterranean provide a stunning backdrop to Marina Grande and the Fishing Harbor, creating an idyllic setting for leisurely strolls and panoramic views. From the harbor's rocky promontory, visitors can gaze out at the sparkling sea and watch as fishing boats bob gently on the waves, their colorful sails a vibrant contrast against the rugged coastline. As the sun sets over the horizon, casting a warm glow upon the waterfront, the scene becomes nothing short of magical, inviting travelers to linger and savor the moment.

Culinary Delights:

No visit to Marina Grande would be complete without sampling the freshest seafood dishes Sorrento has to offer. The harbor's seafood restaurants are renowned for their delectable offerings, ranging from succulent grilled fish and creamy seafood risotto to tender calamari and plump mussels. Diners can savor their meal al fresco on the waterfront terrace, soaking in the tranquil ambiance and savoring the flavors of the sea.

Activities and Attractions:

In addition to dining and sightseeing, Marina Grande and the Fishing Harbor offer a variety of activities to suit every interest. Visitors can take a leisurely boat tour along the coastline, exploring hidden coves and sea caves, or try their hand at fishing with a local guide. For those seeking relaxation, the harbor's sandy beach provides the perfect spot to soak up the Mediterranean sun and take a refreshing dip in the crystal-clear waters.

Practical Information:

- Comfortable footwear is recommended for exploring Marina Grande's cobblestone streets and rocky shoreline.
- Visitors should bring sunscreen and a hat to protect against the sun's rays, especially during the peak summer months.
- While there is no entry fee to visit Marina Grande and the Fishing Harbor, some activities such as boat tours and fishing charters may incur an additional cost.
- The best time to visit is during the early morning or late afternoon, when the harbor is bathed in golden light and the crowds are smaller.

Marina Grande and the Fishing Harbor offer a captivating blend of history, culture, and natural beauty that make them must-see destinations for visitors to Sorrento. Whether you're exploring the cobblestone streets of the fishing village, savoring fresh seafood overlooking the harbor, or simply soaking in the Mediterranean sun, these waterfront gems promise an unforgettable experience that will leave a lasting impression on all who visit. So pack your bags, set sail for Sorrento, and prepare to embark on a journey of discovery along the scenic shores of Marina Grande and the Fishing Harbor.

4.3. Cathedral of Sorrento and Religious Sites

Nestled amidst the charming streets of Sorrento lies a treasure trove of religious and architectural wonders, beckoning travelers from far and wide to experience the spiritual and cultural heritage of this enchanting town. At the forefront of Sorrento's religious landscape stands the Cathedral of Sorrento, a majestic testament to centuries of faith and devotion, alongside other revered religious sites that dot the town's picturesque landscape.

The Cathedral of Sorrento:

Situated in the heart of the Historic Center, the Cathedral of Sorrento, also known as the Duomo di Sorrento, is a magnificent blend of architectural styles that dates back to the 11th century. As visitors approach its grand facade, adorned with intricate marble carvings and towering bell towers, they are immediately enveloped in an aura of reverence and awe.

Upon entering the cathedral, visitors are greeted by a breathtaking interior adorned with stunning frescoes, ornate altars, and exquisite marble sculptures. The highlight of the cathedral is undoubtedly the "Corpo di San Antonino," the relic of Saint Antoninus, the patron saint of Sorrento, which is housed in a silver urn beneath the main altar. Pilgrims and visitors alike flock to the cathedral to pay homage to this revered saint and seek blessings for health and prosperity.

Other Religious Sites in Sorrento:

In addition to the Cathedral of Sorrento, the town is home to a myriad of other religious sites that offer a glimpse into its spiritual and cultural heritage. The Church of San Francesco, located near Piazza Tasso, features a stunning cloister adorned with majolica tiles and offers a peaceful retreat from the bustling streets of the town center. Meanwhile, the Basilica di Sant'Antonino, dedicated to the town's patron saint, houses precious relics and artwork that showcase the deep-rooted devotion of Sorrento's inhabitants.

Why It's Worth Visiting:

A visit to the Cathedral of Sorrento and other religious sites offers a unique opportunity to immerse oneself in the rich tapestry of Sorrento's history, culture, and spirituality. Whether you're drawn to the awe-inspiring architecture, the serene atmosphere of prayer and reflection, or the chance to witness centuries-old traditions come to life, these sacred sites promise an unforgettable journey of discovery and enlightenment.

Practical Information for Visitors:

When planning a visit to the Cathedral of Sorrento and other religious sites, it's important to dress modestly out of respect for the sacredness of these places. Additionally, visitors should check the opening hours of the cathedral and other religious sites in advance, as they may vary depending on the season and religious holidays. Guided tours are often available, providing valuable insights into the history and significance of these revered landmarks.

The Cathedral of Sorrento and religious sites scattered throughout the town stand as must-see attractions that offer a glimpse into Sorrento's spiritual and cultural heritage. Whether you're a devout pilgrim seeking solace and blessings or a curious traveler eager to uncover the secrets of centuries past, these sacred sites invite you to embark on a journey of discovery and contemplation that will leave a lasting impression on your soul. So, come and experience the timeless beauty and profound spirituality of Sorrento's religious landmarks, and let their sacredness inspire and uplift you on your travels.

4.4. Museo Correale and Art Galleries

Sorrento is not only a destination renowned for its breathtaking landscapes but also a hub of artistic inspiration. From ancient artifacts to contemporary masterpieces, the city boasts a rich cultural heritage waiting to be explored. Among the myriad attractions, Museo Correale and other art galleries stand out as must-see destinations for any visitor eager to immerse themselves in Sorrento's vibrant art scene. Let's embark on an enriching journey through these cultural treasures, each offering a unique perspective on the city's artistic legacy.

1. Museo Correale: Where Art Meets History in Splendor

Situated atop a hill overlooking the Gulf of Naples, Museo Correale is a testament to Sorrento's rich cultural heritage. Housed within a majestic neoclassical villa, this museum showcases an extensive collection of paintings, sculptures, ceramics, and decorative arts amassed by the noble Correale di Terranova family over centuries.

Location: Via Correale, 50, 80067 Sorrento NA, Italy

How to Get There: Museo Correale is conveniently located within walking distance from Sorrento's city center. Visitors can also opt for a leisurely stroll or take a short taxi ride from the main square.

Entry Fee: Admission fees vary depending on exhibitions and special events. Typically, the standard admission fee is around €8, with discounts available for students, seniors, and groups. It's advisable to check the museum's website for the latest pricing information.

Why Visit: Museo Correale offers a captivating journey through Sorrento's artistic and cultural heritage, with highlights including works by Luca Giordano, Salvator Rosa, and Giuseppe De Nittis. The museum's exquisite collection, housed within the opulent surroundings of a historic villa, provides a fascinating insight into the city's aristocratic past and artistic legacy.

What to Do: Explore the museum's rich collection of paintings, sculptures, and decorative arts spanning from the Renaissance to the Neoclassical era. Take a leisurely stroll through the villa's lush gardens and enjoy panoramic views of the Bay of Naples from the terrace. Don't forget to visit the museum shop, where you can purchase unique souvenirs and art books to commemorate your visit.

2. Chiostro di San Francesco: A Serene Sanctuary of Art

Tucked away in the heart of Sorrento's historic center, Chiostro di San Francesco offers a tranquil oasis for art lovers seeking refuge from the bustling streets. This ancient cloister, dating back to the 14th century, showcases a rotating selection of contemporary art exhibitions and cultural events.

Location: Piazza Francesco Saverio Gargiulo, 2, 80067 Sorrento NA, Italy

How to Get There: Chiostro di San Francesco is conveniently located near Sorrento's main attractions and can be easily reached on foot from the city center. Visitors can also opt for public transportation or taxis if preferred.

Entry Fee: Admission to Chiostro di San Francesco is typically free of charge, though donations are appreciated to support the maintenance of this historic site.

Why Visit: Chiostro di San Francesco offers a unique blend of history, art, and spirituality within the tranquil confines of a medieval cloister. Whether you're drawn to contemporary art exhibitions or simply seeking a moment of contemplation amidst ancient surroundings, this hidden gem is sure to leave a lasting impression.

What to Do: Explore the cloister's serene courtyard and admire its architectural features, including graceful columns and ornate arches. Take time to peruse the current art exhibition, which showcases the work of local and international artists. Attend a cultural event or musical performance hosted within the cloister's historic walls for a truly immersive experience.

3. Fondazione Sorrento: A Hub of Artistic Innovation

Dedicated to promoting Sorrento's artistic heritage, Fondazione Sorrento serves as a dynamic cultural hub showcasing the talents of local artists and craftsmen. Housed within a historic building in the heart of the city, the foundation hosts a diverse range of exhibitions, workshops, and cultural events throughout the year.

Location: Via Luigi De Maio, 35, 80067 Sorrento NA, Italy

How to Get There: Fondazione Sorrento is centrally located and easily accessible on foot from Sorrento's main attractions. Visitors can also opt for public transportation or taxis if preferred.

Entry Fee: Admission to Fondazione Sorrento may vary depending on exhibitions and events. Some exhibitions may be free, while others may require a nominal fee. It's advisable to check the foundation's website for up-to-date information on pricing and opening hours.

Why Visit: Fondazione Sorrento offers a vibrant platform for emerging and established artists to showcase their work, providing visitors with a glimpse into the city's thriving arts scene. Whether you're interested in painting, sculpture, or traditional crafts, the foundation's diverse programming has something for everyone to enjoy.

What to Do: Explore the foundation's current exhibitions, which feature a wide range of artistic styles and mediums. Attend a workshop or artist talk to gain insight into the creative process behind the works on display. Don't forget to browse the foundation's gift shop, where you can purchase unique souvenirs and handmade crafts by local artisans.

4. Museo Bottega della Tarsia Lignea: A Celebration of Wood Inlay

Located within a historic palazzo overlooking Sorrento's bustling streets, Museo Bottega della Tarsia Lignea offers a fascinating glimpse into the ancient art of wood inlay, or marquetry. This unique museum showcases exquisite examples of Sorrentine marquetry, a traditional craft dating back to the Renaissance. **Location:** Via San Nicola, 28, 80067 Sorrento NA, Italy

How to Get There: Museo Bottega della Tarsia Lignea is situated near Sorrento's city center and can be easily reached on foot or by public transportation. Visitors can also opt for a taxi if preferred.

Entry Fee: Admission to Museo Bottega della Tarsia Lignea is typically free of charge, though donations are appreciated to support the museum's conservation efforts.

Why Visit: Whether you're a woodworking enthusiast or simply appreciate fine craftsmanship, Museo Bottega della Tarsia Lignea offers a unique opportunity to explore Sorrento's rich heritage of wood inlay. Visitors can admire intricate designs, learn about traditional marquetry techniques, and even try their hand at creating their own masterpiece in the museum's interactive workshops.

What to Do: Marvel at the museum's stunning collection of wood inlay furniture, boxes, and decorative objects, which showcase the skill and artistry of Sorrento's master craftsmen. Participate in a guided tour or workshop to gain insight into the history and techniques of marquetry. Don't miss the opportunity to browse the museum's gift shop, where you can purchase handmade wood inlay souvenirs to commemorate your visit.

5. Museo Correale di Terranova: A Cultural Gem in Sorrento's Crown

Set amidst scenic gardens overlooking the Bay of Naples, Museo Correale di Terranova offers a comprehensive overview of Sorrento's cultural heritage. This esteemed museum showcases a diverse array of artworks and artifacts spanning millennia, providing visitors with a captivating journey through the city's history and artistic legacy.

Location: Via Correale, 50, 80067 Sorrento NA, Italy

How to Get There: Museo Correale di Terranova is centrally located in Sorrento and can be easily reached on foot or by public transportation from the city center. Visitors can also opt for a taxi if preferred.

Entry Fee: Admission fees to Museo Correale di Terranova may vary depending on exhibitions and special events. It's advisable to check the museum's website for up-to-date pricing information.

Why Visit: Museo Correale di Terranova offers an immersive experience for visitors eager to explore Sorrento's rich cultural heritage. From ancient Roman artifacts to contemporary art installations, the museum's diverse collection provides insight into the city's past and present. Plus, the scenic surroundings of the villa and gardens offer a picturesque backdrop for exploration and relaxation.

What to Do: Explore the museum's extensive collection of paintings, sculptures, ceramics, and decorative arts, which span from antiquity to the present day. Take a leisurely stroll through the villa's lush gardens and enjoy panoramic views of the Bay of Naples from its terrace. Don't forget to visit the museum's gift shop, where you can purchase unique souvenirs and art books to commemorate your visit.

Practical Information for Visitors:
Opening Hours: The opening hours of Sorrento's art galleries and museums may vary depending on the season and any ongoing exhibitions or events. It's advisable to check the individual websites or contact the venues directly for up-to-date information on opening hours.

Accessibility: Most of Sorrento's art galleries and museums are wheelchair accessible, though some historic buildings may have limited accessibility. Visitors with mobility concerns are encouraged to contact the venues in advance to inquire about accessibility features and accommodations.

Guided Tours: Many of Sorrento's art galleries and museums offer guided tours led by knowledgeable docents, providing visitors with deeper insights into the exhibits and their historical significance. Consider joining a guided tour to enhance your experience and gain a greater appreciation for Sorrento's cultural heritage.

Photography: While photography is generally permitted in Sorrento's art galleries and museums, it's advisable to respect any restrictions or guidelines provided by the venue. Be sure to capture your favorite moments and artworks to treasure as lasting memories of your visit.

Sorrento's art galleries and museums offer a diverse and enriching array of experiences for visitors eager to explore the city's cultural heritage. From ancient artifacts to contemporary masterpieces, these cultural treasures provide insight into Sorrento's rich history, artistic legacy, and vibrant creative community. Whether you're drawn to classical art, modern sculpture, or traditional crafts, there's something for everyone to discover and enjoy in Sorrento's vibrant cultural scene. So, why wait? Embark on an artistic journey through Sorrento's storied past and vibrant present, and let the city's cultural treasures inspire and delight you.

4.5. Villa Comunale and Panoramic Views

Nestled atop the cliffs overlooking the Mediterranean, Villa Comunale is a tranquil oasis in the heart of Sorrento. Originally built as a private estate in the 19th century, the villa's lush gardens and panoramic views have made it a beloved gathering place for locals and visitors alike. Villa Comunale offers a serene retreat from the bustling streets of Sorrento, with its manicured gardens, shady pathways, and panoramic terraces providing the perfect backdrop for relaxation and contemplation. Whether enjoying a leisurely stroll, admiring the views of the Bay of Naples, or picnicking amidst the verdant surroundings, Villa Comunale offers something for everyone to enjoy.

Punta del Capo: A Cliffside Retreat with Unparalleled Views

Located on the western edge of Sorrento, Punta del Capo offers visitors a secluded retreat with unparalleled views of the Gulf of Naples and the Amalfi Coast. This cliffside promontory is home to the ruins of an ancient Roman villa, as well as a scenic walking path that winds along the coastline, offering panoramic views of the sea and surrounding landscape. Punta del Capo offers a peaceful escape from the crowds of Sorrento, with its rugged cliffs, tranquil coves, and sweeping views providing the perfect backdrop for relaxation and exploration. Whether hiking along the coastal path, sunbathing on the rocky shores, or simply soaking in the natural beauty of the surroundings, Punta del Capo offers a truly unforgettable experience.

Villa Fiorentino: A Garden Paradise with Panoramic Vistas

Perched atop the cliffs overlooking Sorrento's historic center, Villa Fiorentino is a hidden gem waiting to be discovered. This elegant villa is surrounded by lush gardens and terraces offering panoramic views of the city, the sea, and the distant peaks of the Amalfi Coast. Villa Fiorentino offers a tranquil retreat from the hustle and bustle of Sorrento, with its verdant gardens, shady pathways, and panoramic terraces providing the perfect setting for relaxation and contemplation. Whether exploring the villa's historic architecture, admiring the views of the Bay of Naples, or simply enjoying a leisurely stroll amidst the fragrant flowers and lush greenery, Villa Fiorentino offers a serene escape from the ordinary.

Marina Grande: A Charming Fishing Village with Scenic Views

Tucked away at the base of Sorrento's cliffs, Marina Grande is a picturesque fishing village renowned for its colorful boats, waterfront restaurants, and stunning views of the sea and coastline. Visitors can stroll along the waterfront promenade, relax on the sandy beach, or dine al fresco while soaking in the beauty of the surrounding landscape. Marina Grande offers a charming glimpse into Sorrento's maritime heritage, with its bustling harbor, colorful fishing boats, and waterfront cafes creating a vibrant and lively atmosphere. Whether sampling fresh seafood, browsing the local shops, or simply enjoying a leisurely stroll along the waterfront, Marina Grande offers a quintessentially Sorrentine experience that is not to be missed.

Sorrento Cathedral: A Historic Landmark with Panoramic Views

Perched atop a cliff overlooking Sorrento's historic center, the Cathedral of Saints Philip and James offers visitors a unique vantage point from which to admire the city's panoramic vistas. The cathedral's bell tower, accessible via a narrow staircase, provides sweeping views of the city, the sea, and the surrounding landscape, making it a popular destination for photography enthusiasts and sightseers alike. Sorrento Cathedral offers a fascinating glimpse into the city's religious and architectural heritage, with its ornate facades, elegant interiors, and panoramic views providing a captivating backdrop for exploration and contemplation. Whether admiring the cathedral's art and architecture, attending a religious service, or simply enjoying the views from the bell tower, Sorrento Cathedral offers a memorable experience for visitors of all ages.

Mount Vesuvius: A Majestic Volcano with Unforgettable Views

Standing tall on the horizon overlooking Sorrento, Mount Vesuvius offers visitors a once-in-a-lifetime opportunity to witness the power and beauty of one of the world's most iconic volcanoes. A guided tour to the summit of Mount Vesuvius promises breathtaking views of the surrounding landscape, including the Bay of Naples, the Amalfi Coast, and the ruins of Pompeii, making it an unforgettable experience for nature lovers and adventure seekers alike. Mount Vesuvius offers a unique opportunity to witness the raw power and beauty of one of the world's most famous volcanoes, with its rugged slopes, steaming vents, and panoramic views providing a truly unforgettable experience. Whether hiking to the summit, exploring the crater, or simply admiring the views from afar, Mount Vesuvius offers a thrilling adventure that is sure to leave a lasting impression.

In conclusion, Sorrento's Villa Comunale and five panoramic views offer visitors a captivating glimpse into the city's natural beauty and cultural heritage. Whether exploring the verdant gardens of Villa Comunale, admiring the sweeping vistas of Punta del Capo, or witnessing the power of Mount Vesuvius, each destination promises an unforgettable experience that is sure to leave a lasting impression.

CHAPTER 5

PRACTICAL INFORMATION AND TRAVEL RESOURCES

5.1 Maps and Navigation

***Click the link or Scan the QR Code with a device to view a comprehensive map of Sorrento –** https://shorturl.at/sIKMV*

Sorrento, with its breathtaking vistas overlooking the Bay of Naples and Mount Vesuvius, is a dream destination for travelers seeking a blend of rich history, stunning landscapes, and Mediterranean charm. As you embark on your journey to this enchanting Italian town, navigating its winding streets and discovering its hidden gems becomes an integral part of your experience. In this guide, we'll explore the various methods of navigation available to you, from traditional paper maps to digital resources, ensuring that you make the most of your time in Sorrento.

Sorrento Tourist Map: Your Trusty Companion

Before delving into the digital realm, let's first familiarize ourselves with the traditional method of navigation: the Sorrento tourist map. Available at information centers, hotels, and tourist hotspots throughout the town, these maps offer a tangible, easy-to-use guide to Sorrento's attractions, streets, and landmarks. With detailed illustrations and labeled points of interest, they provide a sense of orientation that digital maps sometimes lack. Whether you're strolling through the historic center or planning a day trip along the stunning Amalfi Coast, a Sorrento tourist map ensures that you never lose your way.

Accessing Offline Maps in Sorrento

For those moments when Wi-Fi signals waver and data connections falter, having an offline map on hand can be a lifesaver. In Sorrento, obtaining a paper map is as simple as visiting a local tourist information center, hotel concierge, or even a nearby bookstore. These maps are often free of charge and come with handy tips for navigating the town's narrow streets and alleyways. Additionally, many souvenir shops offer beautifully illustrated maps that serve as keepsakes of your Sorrento adventure. By keeping a physical map in your pocket or backpack, you'll always have a reliable navigation tool at your fingertips, regardless of internet availability.

Embracing Digital Navigation: The Key to Seamless Exploration

In today's digital age, smartphones and tablets have revolutionized the way we navigate unfamiliar terrain. Sorrento is no exception, with a plethora of digital mapping tools at your disposal. One of the most popular options is Google Maps, which provides real-time navigation, detailed street views, and information on public transportation options. By simply downloading the Google Maps app and pre-loading maps for offline use, you can navigate Sorrento with ease, even without an internet connection.

Exploring Sorrento's Digital Maps: A Click Away

In addition to mainstream mapping apps, Sorrento offers its own digital maps tailored to the needs of travelers. By clicking on the link or scanning the QR code provided in your travel guide, you gain access to a comprehensive map of Sorrento, complete with insider tips, suggested itineraries, and interactive features. This digital resource serves as your virtual guide to the town, allowing you to explore its attractions, dining options, and hidden gems with confidence. Whether you're seeking the perfect gelato spot or searching for the best vantage point to watch the sunset, Sorrento's digital map has you covered.

Tips for Using Digital Maps Effectively

While digital maps offer unparalleled convenience, maximizing their utility requires a few simple tips:

Download Maps for Offline Use: Before setting out on your adventures, download offline maps of Sorrento to ensure uninterrupted navigation, especially in areas with spotty network coverage.

Enable Location Services: Allow your device to access your location for accurate positioning on the map, making it easier to navigate streets and landmarks.

Explore Points of Interest: Take advantage of the interactive features offered by digital maps to discover hidden gems and must-see attractions in Sorrento.

Stay Charged: Ensure that your device is fully charged or carry a portable charger to prevent unexpected battery drain while using digital maps throughout the day.

In Sorrento, the journey is as enchanting as the destination itself, and navigating its charming streets and scenic vistas is a delightful adventure in its own right. Whether you prefer the tactile experience of a paper map or the convenience of digital navigation, Sorrento offers a multitude of resources to guide you on your exploration. By embracing both traditional and modern mapping methods, you'll uncover the beauty and allure of this coastal gem, creating memories to last a lifetime. So pack your bags, grab your map, and get ready to embark on a journey of discovery in the heart of southern Italy. Buon viaggio!

5.2 Essential Packing List

Packing for a trip to Sorrento requires careful consideration to ensure you have everything you need for a comfortable and enjoyable stay. From exploring the charming streets of the town to soaking up the sun along the Amalfi Coast, being prepared with the right essentials will enhance your experience in this enchanting destination.

Clothing

When it comes to clothing, Sorrento's climate and activities influence what you should pack. Summers are warm and sunny, so lightweight and breathable clothing is essential. Pack comfortable walking shoes for exploring the town's cobblestone streets and sturdy sandals for beach days. Don't forget to bring swimwear, sunglasses, and a wide-brimmed hat for protection from the sun. While Sorrento tends to be more casual, you may want to pack some dressier outfits for dining out in the evenings or visiting upscale establishments.

Weather Considerations

While Sorrento enjoys mild winters, it's essential to be prepared for occasional rain and cooler temperatures, especially if you're visiting during the shoulder seasons. Pack a lightweight waterproof jacket or umbrella, as well as layers like sweaters or cardigans, to stay comfortable during cooler evenings. Checking the weather forecast before your trip can help you pack accordingly and ensure you're prepared for any unexpected changes in weather.

Sun Protection and Essentials

With its Mediterranean climate, Sorrento experiences plenty of sunshine throughout the year. To protect your skin from harmful UV rays, be sure to pack sunscreen with a high SPF, as well as lip balm with SPF protection. Additionally, bring a refillable water bottle to stay hydrated while exploring the town and its surroundings. Consider packing a small first-aid kit with essentials like bandaids, pain relievers, and insect repellent to address any minor injuries or discomfort during your travels.

Travel Accessories

To make your visit to Sorrento more convenient and enjoyable, consider packing a few essential travel accessories. A lightweight backpack or tote bag is perfect for carrying your essentials while exploring the town or embarking on day trips. Don't forget to bring a portable phone charger or power bank to keep your devices charged while on the go. If you plan on visiting historical sites or museums, consider packing a travel guide or map to help you navigate and learn more about Sorrento's rich history and culture.

Miscellaneous Items

In addition to the essentials mentioned above, there are a few miscellaneous items worth considering for your trip to Sorrento. Pack a reusable shopping bag for picking up souvenirs or groceries during your stay. If you plan on dining out, consider bringing a reusable utensil set to reduce waste and minimize your environmental impact. Finally, don't forget to pack any necessary travel documents, such as your passport, ID, travel insurance information, and itinerary, to ensure a smooth and hassle-free trip.

Packing for a trip to Sorrento requires careful consideration of the destination's climate, activities, and your personal preferences. By packing essential clothing, weather-appropriate gear, sun protection, travel accessories, and miscellaneous items, you'll be well-prepared to enjoy all that Sorrento has to offer. Whether you're exploring the town's historic sites, lounging on the beach, or indulging in delicious Italian cuisine, having the right essentials on hand will ensure a comfortable and memorable visit to this enchanting destination.

5.3 Visa Requirements and Entry Procedures

Traveling to Sorrento, the charming coastal town in Italy, is a dream for many visitors seeking a picturesque Mediterranean getaway. For most travelers, entry into Sorrento will require ensuring proper visa documentation and understanding entry procedures. Fortunately, navigating these requirements is relatively straightforward for citizens of many countries.

Visa Requirements

Before planning your trip to Sorrento, it's essential to check if you require a visa to enter Italy. Citizens of the European Union, the United States, Canada, Australia, and many other countries typically do not need a visa for short stays (up to 90 days) for tourism purposes. However, it's always wise to check the latest visa regulations on the official website of the Italian consulate or embassy in your country.

For those who require a visa, the application process typically involves providing necessary documentation, such as a passport, proof of accommodation, travel itinerary, and sufficient funds for the duration of your stay. Processing times can vary, so it's advisable to apply well in advance of your planned travel dates.

Entry Procedures by Air Travel
Flying into Sorrento is a convenient option for international visitors. The nearest major airport is Naples International Airport (NAP), located approximately 50 kilometers north of Sorrento. Upon arrival at Naples Airport, travelers can easily reach Sorrento by various modes of transportation, including train, bus, or private transfer.

Entry Procedures by Train
For travelers arriving in Italy from other European cities, train travel is an efficient and scenic option. Italy's extensive rail network connects major cities to smaller towns like Sorrento. Visitors can take a train from cities like Rome or Naples to reach Sorrento. The Circumvesuviana train line offers direct services from Naples to Sorrento, with a journey time of approximately one hour.

Entry Procedures by Road
Driving to Sorrento provides the flexibility to explore the stunning Amalfi Coast at your own pace. The town is accessible by car via the A3 motorway, with well-marked signs directing travelers to Sorrento. However, it's worth noting that navigating the narrow and winding coastal roads can be challenging, especially during peak tourist seasons.

Airlines and Ticketing Options
Several airlines operate flights to Naples International Airport, providing travelers with a range of options to reach Sorrento.

Alitalia: Italy's national carrier, Alitalia, offers direct flights to Naples from major cities worldwide. Travelers can book flights and manage reservations conveniently through the Alitalia website or mobile app. For bookings visit: (https://www.ita-airways.com/en_en).

Lufthansa: As one of Europe's largest airlines, Lufthansa provides flights to Naples with connections through its hub airports such as Frankfurt and Munich. Tickets can be purchased online via the Lufthansa website or through authorized travel agencies. For bookings visit: (https://www.lufthansa.com/ng/en/homepage).

British Airways: For travelers originating from the UK or other international destinations, British Airways offers flights to Naples with convenient connections at London Heathrow Airport. Booking flights with British Airways is straightforward via their website or mobile app. For bookings visit: (https://shorturl.at/fGJS2).

Ryanair: Known for its budget-friendly fares, Ryanair operates flights to Naples from various European cities. Travelers can find competitive ticket prices and book directly on the Ryanair website or mobile app. For bookings visit: (https://www.ryanair.com/ie/en).

EasyJet: Another popular budget airline, EasyJet, serves Naples Airport with flights from several European destinations. Booking tickets with EasyJet can be done online, offering flexibility in choosing travel dates and fares. For bookings visit: (https://shorturl.at/wQW07).

Delta Air Lines: For travelers from North America, Delta Air Lines offers connections to Naples via its partner airlines and hubs such as Amsterdam, Paris, or New York-JFK. Tickets can be purchased through the Delta website or authorized travel agents. For bookings visit: (https://www.delta.com/).

Whether arriving by air, train, or road, visitors to Sorrento are greeted with stunning views of the Mediterranean coastline and warm Italian hospitality. Understanding visa requirements, entry procedures, and transportation options ensures a smooth and enjoyable journey to this enchanting destination. With a myriad of airlines serving Naples International Airport, travelers can find convenient flights and book tickets easily, making Sorrento accessible from virtually anywhere in the world.

5.4 Safety Tips and Emergency Contacts

Ensuring safety during your visit to Sorrento is paramount to enjoying a memorable and worry-free experience. From navigating the bustling streets to exploring the stunning coastal landscapes, understanding safety tips and knowing emergency contacts can help travelers stay prepared for any situation.

Safety Tips

Stay Vigilant in Crowded Areas: Like any popular tourist destination, Sorrento can get crowded, especially during peak seasons. Keep your belongings secure and be mindful of your surroundings to avoid pickpocketing incidents.

Use Reliable Transportation: Opt for licensed taxis or reputable car rental services when exploring Sorrento and its surrounding areas. Avoid unlicensed taxis to ensure your safety and prevent potential scams.

Watch Your Step: The narrow streets and uneven pathways in Sorrento can pose tripping hazards, particularly for elderly or mobility-impaired visitors. Watch your step and wear comfortable footwear suitable for walking on various surfaces.

Stay Hydrated and Sun-Protected: The Mediterranean climate in Sorrento can be hot and sunny, especially in the summer months. Stay hydrated by drinking plenty of water and apply sunscreen regularly to protect your skin from sunburn.

Respect Local Customs and Laws: Familiarize yourself with Italian customs and laws to avoid inadvertently offending locals or getting into legal trouble. Dress modestly when visiting religious sites and adhere to local regulations, such as no smoking zones.

Be Cautious Near Cliffs and Beaches: While Sorrento's coastline offers breathtaking views, exercise caution when walking near cliffs or swimming in the sea. Pay attention to warning signs and avoid risky behaviors to prevent accidents or injuries.

Emergency Contacts

Emergency Services: In case of emergencies requiring police, ambulance, or fire services, dial 112 from any phone in Italy. This universal emergency number connects you to the appropriate authorities for immediate assistance.

Local Police (Polizia Locale): For non-emergency situations or to report minor incidents, contact the local police station in Sorrento. They can provide assistance with lost property, minor accidents, or general inquiries related to safety and security.

Medical Assistance: If you require medical assistance or urgent healthcare services during your stay in Sorrento, seek help from local hospitals or medical clinics. The nearest hospital to Sorrento is the Hospital of Sorrento (Ospedale di Sorrento), located on Via San Bartolomeo.

Consular Assistance: Travelers from foreign countries can seek consular assistance from their respective embassies or consulates in Italy. Consular services may include passport replacement, legal assistance, or support in case of emergencies.

Roadside Assistance: If you encounter vehicle-related issues or breakdowns while driving in Sorrento or its surrounding areas, contact local roadside assistance services for help. Car rental companies often provide roadside assistance as part of their services.

Coast Guard (Guardia Costiera): For emergencies at sea or coastal areas, including water-related accidents or distress signals, contact the Italian Coast Guard. They can coordinate search and rescue operations and provide assistance to individuals in distress.

By following safety tips and knowing essential emergency contacts, travelers can enjoy a safe and enjoyable visit to Sorrento. Whether exploring the town's historic streets, indulging in delicious Italian cuisine, or admiring the breathtaking views of the Amalfi Coast, being prepared for any situation enhances the overall travel experience. With proper precautions and access to emergency services, visitors can relax and immerse themselves in the beauty and charm of Sorrento with peace of mind.

5.5 Currency, Banking, Budgeting and Money Matters

Ensuring financial preparedness is essential for a seamless and enjoyable visit to Sorrento, Italy. Understanding the currency, banking options, budgeting tips, and accessing money exchange services are crucial aspects of planning your trip to this picturesque coastal town.

Currency and Exchange Rates

The official currency of Italy is the Euro (EUR), denoted by the symbol €. Euro banknotes come in denominations of €5, €10, €20, €50, €100, €200, and €500, while coins are available in values of 1, 2, 5, 10, 20, and 50 cents, as well as €1 and €2. Before traveling to Sorrento, it's advisable to check the latest exchange rates to ensure you get the best value for your money.

Banking Services

Sorrento offers various banking services to cater to the needs of visitors. Several banks operate in the town, providing a range of financial products and services, including currency exchange, ATM withdrawals, and international money transfers. Some prominent banks in Sorrento include:

Banca Intesa Sanpaolo: Located at Via Degli Aranci, 10, Banca Intesa Sanpaolo offers comprehensive banking services, including currency exchange and ATM facilities. Visitors can access their accounts or exchange currency conveniently at this branch.

UniCredit Bank: UniCredit Bank has a branch at Corso Italia, 264, offering banking services such as currency exchange, ATM withdrawals, and assistance with international transactions. The branch is easily accessible in the heart of Sorrento.

BNL Gruppo BNP Paribas: Situated at Via degli Aranci, 48, BNL Gruppo BNP Paribas provides banking services tailored to the needs of tourists, including currency exchange and assistance with financial transactions.

Banca Monte dei Paschi di Siena: With a branch at Via Luigi De Maio, 34, Banca Monte dei Paschi di Siena offers banking services, including currency exchange, ATM facilities, and personalized financial advice for visitors to Sorrento.

Cassa di Risparmio di Firenze (Carifirenze): Carifirenze operates a branch at Via Luigi De Maio, 40, providing banking services such as currency exchange, ATM withdrawals, and assistance with financial transactions for tourists and residents alike.

Credito Emiliano (Credem): Credem has a branch located at Piazza Tasso, 41, offering banking services tailored to the needs of visitors to Sorrento. Services include currency exchange, ATM facilities, and personalized financial solutions.

Currency Exchange Services

In addition to banks, visitors to Sorrento can access currency exchange services through bureaus de change located throughout the town. These establishments offer competitive exchange rates and convenient locations for exchanging foreign currency into euros. Some notable bureaus de change in Sorrento include:

Change Express: Located at Via degli Aranci, 78, Change Express provides currency exchange services for various currencies, including US dollars, British pounds, and Japanese yen.

Money Exchange Sorrento: Situated at Piazza Tasso, 4, Money Exchange Sorrento offers currency exchange services and competitive rates for visitors needing to convert foreign currency into euros.

Global Exchange: Global Exchange operates a branch at Via degli Aranci, 75, providing currency exchange services for travelers with a wide range of currencies and convenient opening hours.

Forexchange: Forexchange has a branch at Corso Italia, 19, offering currency exchange services and assistance with foreign currency transactions for visitors to Sorrento.

Sorrento Change: Sorrento Change is located at Via degli Aranci, 65, and provides currency exchange services for tourists needing to convert foreign currency into euros or vice versa.

Eurochange: Eurochange operates a branch at Via degli Aranci, 45, offering currency exchange services and competitive rates for visitors exchanging foreign currency in Sorrento.

Budgeting Tips

When planning your budget for a visit to Sorrento, consider the following tips to make the most of your money: Research average costs for accommodations, dining, transportation, and activities in Sorrento to estimate your daily expenses. Take advantage of free or low-cost attractions, such as exploring the town's historic streets, visiting local markets, and enjoying scenic walks along the coastline. Consider purchasing a Sorrento Card or other tourist passes that offer discounts on attractions, transportation, and dining for additional savings. Look for budget-friendly dining options, such as local trattorias and pizzerias, where you can enjoy authentic Italian cuisine without breaking the bank. Finally, plan your excursions and day trips in advance to take advantage of any early booking discounts or special promotions offered by tour operators.

By understanding currency, banking options, budgeting tips, and accessing currency exchange services, visitors can effectively manage their finances and enjoy a stress-free visit to Sorrento. Whether exchanging currency at banks or bureaus de change, withdrawing cash from ATMs, or budgeting wisely for accommodations and activities, being financially prepared enhances the overall travel experience in this enchanting coastal town.

5.6 Language, Communication and Useful Phrases

Understanding the local language and communication customs can greatly enhance your experience while visiting Sorrento, Italy. While Italian is the official language spoken in Sorrento, many locals also understand and speak English, especially in tourist areas. However, learning some basic Italian phrases and communication tips can help you navigate the town more effectively and interact with locals in a meaningful way.

Language in Sorrento:

Italian is the primary language spoken in Sorrento, as it is throughout Italy. While English is widely understood, especially in tourist areas, locals appreciate visitors who attempt to communicate in Italian. Embracing the local language can also enrich your cultural experience and foster connections with the community.

Useful Phrases

Greetings

- *Buongiorno (Good morning)*

- *Buonasera (Good evening)*

- *Buon pomeriggio (Good afternoon)*

- *Ciao (Hello/Goodbye)*

- *Arrivederci (Goodbye)*

Common Courtesies

- *Grazie (Thank you)*

- *Prego (You're welcome)*

- *Per favore (Please)*

- *Scusa (Excuse me)*

- *Mi dispiace (I'm sorry)*

Basic Questions

- *Come stai? (How are you?)*

- *Quanto costa? (How much does it cost?)*

- *Dove si trova...? (Where is...?)*

- *Posso avere...? (Can I have...?)*

- *Parli inglese? (Do you speak English?)*

Navigating

- *Dov'è la stazione dei treni/autobus? (Where is the train/bus station?)*

- *Vorrei prenotare un tavolo per due, per favore. (I would like to book a table for two, please.)*

- *Quanto tempo ci vuole per arrivare a...? (How long does it take to get to...?)*

- Sto cercando un hotel. (I'm looking for a hotel.)

Dining

- Vorrei ordinare... (I would like to order...)

- Un bicchiere di vino rosso/bianco, per favore. (A glass of red/white wine, please.)

- Il conto, per favore. (The bill, please.)

- Questo è delizioso! (This is delicious!)

Communication Tips

Taking the time to learn a few basic Italian phrases can go a long way in Sorrento. Locals appreciate the effort, and it can help facilitate smoother interactions, especially in less touristy areas. When speaking English, especially if the person you're communicating with has limited proficiency, speak slowly and clearly to ensure understanding. Italians are known for their expressive gestures and body language. Incorporating gestures can help convey your message more effectively and bridge any language barriers. Also, Patience and politeness are valued in Italian culture. If you encounter communication challenges, remain patient and polite, and try to find alternative ways to convey your finally, don't hesitate to ask for help or clarification if you're unsure about something. Locals are generally friendly and willing to assist visitors, especially if you approach them politely.

Mastering some basic Italian phrases and communication tips can greatly enhance your experience while visiting Sorrento. Whether navigating the town, interacting with locals, or dining at local restaurants, effective communication fosters meaningful connections and enriches your cultural immersion. Embrace the opportunity to engage with the local language and culture, and you'll find your experience in Sorrento even more rewarding.

5.7 Useful Websites, Mobile Apps and Online Resources

Planning a trip to Sorrento involves gathering information, booking accommodations, finding activities, and navigating the town efficiently. With the advancement of technology, there are numerous websites, mobile apps, and online resources designed to assist travelers in making the most of their visit to Sorrento.

TripAdvisor

TripAdvisor is a comprehensive travel platform offering reviews, recommendations, and bookings for accommodations, restaurants, attractions, and activities in Sorrento. Visitors can access user-generated reviews, browse photos, and compare prices to make informed decisions about their travel plans using : (*https://shorturl.at/egBN0*) Additionally, the TripAdvisor forums provide a platform for travelers to ask questions and receive advice from experienced visitors and locals alike.

Google Maps: *Available on Google Playstore and Apple store.*

Google Maps is an indispensable tool for navigating Sorrento and its surrounding areas. Visitors can use the app to find directions, locate points of interest, and explore nearby attractions. Google Maps also provides real-time traffic updates, public transportation information, and street views, making it easier for travelers to get around efficiently.

Visit Sorrento

The official website of Visit Sorrento: *(https://www.sorrentoinfo.com/*) offers a wealth of information and resources for planning a trip to the town. Visitors can find details about accommodations, dining options, attractions, events, and transportation services. The website also provides insights into the history, culture, and traditions of Sorrento, helping travelers gain a deeper understanding of the destination.

Rome2rio

Rome2rio is a comprehensive travel planning platform that helps visitors find the best transportation options to and from Sorrento. (*https://www.rome2rio.com/*). The website provides information on flights, trains, buses, ferries, and driving routes, along with estimated travel times and costs. Travelers can use Rome2rio to plan multi-modal journeys, compare different transportation options, and make informed decisions based on their preferences and budget.

Sorrento Coast Limousine Service App: *Available on Google Playstore and Apple store.*

The Sorrento Coast Limousine Service app offers reliable transportation services for visitors to Sorrento and the Amalfi Coast. Travelers can book private transfers, tours, and excursions directly through the app, ensuring hassle-free transportation during their stay. The app also provides real-time updates on the status of bookings and allows users to communicate with customer support for any assistance needed.

MySorrento: *Available on Google Playstore and Apple store.*

MySorrento is a mobile app designed to enhance the visitor experience in Sorrento by providing personalized recommendations and curated experiences. The app offers insights into local attractions, dining options, events, and activities, tailored to the preferences and interests of individual users. With MySorrento, travelers can discover hidden gems, explore off-the-beaten-path destinations, and create memorable experiences during their stay.

Mobile Apps for Intended Visitors: *Available on Google Playstore and Apple store.*

Sorrento Beaches Guide: The Sorrento Beaches Guide app provides information on the best beaches in Sorrento and the surrounding area. Visitors can access details about beach amenities, water quality, nearby attractions, and transportation options, helping them plan enjoyable beach outings during their stay.

Sorrento Foodie: Sorrento Foodie is a mobile app dedicated to culinary experiences in Sorrento. The app features recommendations for local restaurants, cafes, gelaterias, and specialty food shops, along with reviews, menus, and reservation options. Food enthusiasts can use Sorrento Foodie to discover authentic Italian cuisine and culinary delights in the town.

Sorrento Audio Guide: The Sorrento Audio Guide app offers audio-guided tours of Sorrento's landmarks, historical sites, and cultural attractions. Visitors can explore the town at their own pace while listening to narrated descriptions and anecdotes about each location. The app provides an immersive way to learn about Sorrento's rich history and heritage while sightseeing.

Sorrento Shopping Guide: The Sorrento Shopping Guide app helps visitors discover the best shopping destinations in the town, from boutiques and artisan shops to markets and souvenir stores. Users can browse curated lists of shopping venues, explore special offers and discounts, and plan shopping excursions based on their preferences and interests.

Sorrento Events Calendar: The Sorrento Events Calendar app provides information on upcoming events, festivals, concerts, and cultural activities in Sorrento. Visitors can stay updated on the latest happenings in the town, plan their itinerary around featured events, and participate in local celebrations during their visit.

Sorrento Language Translator: The Sorrento Language Translator app helps visitors overcome language barriers by providing translations for common phrases and expressions in Italian. Travelers can use the app to communicate with locals, ask for directions, order food, and engage in basic conversations, enhancing their overall experience in Sorrento.

With the abundance of websites, mobile apps, and online resources available, planning a visit to Sorrento has never been easier. From booking accommodations and finding activities to navigating the town and enhancing cultural experiences, these digital tools offer valuable assistance and insights for travelers. By leveraging technology, visitors can optimize their time, discover hidden gems, and create unforgettable memories during their stay in Sorrento.

5.8 Visitor Centers and Tourist Assistance

When visiting Sorrento, having access to visitor centers and tourist assistance can greatly enhance your experience by providing valuable information, recommendations, and support services. These centers serve as hubs for travelers seeking guidance, assistance, and local insights to make the most of their time in Sorrento.

Visitor Centers

Sorrento Tourist Information Center (Infopoint Sorrento): Located in the heart of Sorrento at Piazza Tasso, the Sorrento Tourist Information Center is a primary resource for visitors seeking information about the town and its surrounding attractions. Staffed by knowledgeable personnel, the center offers maps, brochures, and guidance on accommodations, dining, transportation, and activities. Visitors can also inquire about guided tours, excursions, and special events happening in Sorrento.

Sorrento Peninsula Tourist Office: Situated on Corso Italia, the Sorrento Peninsula Tourist Office provides comprehensive assistance to visitors exploring Sorrento and the wider peninsula. In addition to offering tourist information and assistance with itinerary planning, the office organizes cultural events, exhibitions, and guided tours to showcase the region's rich history and natural beauty.

Sorrento Coast Visitor Center: Located near the Marina Grande, the Sorrento Coast Visitor Center serves as a welcoming point for tourists arriving by sea. Staffed by multilingual personnel, the center offers assistance with boat tours, water sports activities, and coastal excursions. Visitors can also obtain information about nearby beaches, diving spots, and sailing opportunities along the Sorrento coast.

Sant'Agnello Tourist Information Point: Situated in the neighboring town of Sant'Agnello, the Tourist Information Point provides assistance to visitors exploring both Sant'Agnello and Sorrento. Travelers can obtain maps, brochures, and recommendations for accommodations, restaurants, and attractions in the area. The center also offers guidance on public transportation options and day trips to nearby destinations.

Meta di Sorrento Tourist Information Center: Located in the coastal village of Meta di Sorrento, this tourist information center caters to visitors staying in Meta and neighboring areas. Staffed by friendly locals, the center offers assistance with accommodations, transportation, and sightseeing options in Meta and its surroundings. Visitors can also learn about local events, festivals, and cultural activities taking place during their stay.

Vico Equense Tourist Office: Situated in the nearby town of Vico Equense, the Tourist Office provides assistance to visitors exploring the Sorrento Peninsula and the Amalfi Coast. Travelers can receive information about accommodations, dining options, and attractions in Vico Equense, as well as transportation connections to Sorrento and other nearby destinations. The office also offers guided tours and hiking excursions to showcase the natural beauty of the region.

Special Services of Tourist Assistants

Multilingual Assistance: Tourist assistants at visitor centers are often fluent in multiple languages, including English, French, Spanish, and German, among others. This enables them to provide personalized assistance and guidance to visitors from diverse cultural backgrounds.

Customized Itinerary Planning: Tourist assistants can help visitors plan customized itineraries based on their interests, preferences, and available time. Whether you're interested in exploring historical sites, enjoying culinary experiences, or embarking on outdoor adventures, tourist assistants can tailor recommendations to suit your needs.

Booking Services: Visitor centers often offer booking services for accommodations, transportation, guided tours, and cultural activities. Tourist assistants can help you secure reservations, purchase tickets, and arrange logistical details to ensure a seamless and enjoyable experience during your stay in Sorrento.

Local Insights and Recommendations: Tourist assistants are well-versed in the local attractions, hidden gems, and off-the-beaten-path experiences that make Sorrento unique. They can provide insider tips, recommendations, and insights to help you discover the best that Sorrento has to offer, beyond the typical tourist hotspots.

Emergency Assistance: In addition to providing tourist information, visitor centers also offer assistance in case of emergencies. Tourist assistants can offer guidance and support in situations such as lost belongings, medical emergencies, or unexpected travel disruptions, ensuring that visitors receive timely assistance and support when needed.

Cultural Events and Activities: Tourist assistants keep visitors informed about upcoming cultural events, festivals, and activities happening in Sorrento. Whether it's a local music concert, art exhibition, or traditional festival, tourist assistants can provide information about cultural happenings that allow visitors to immerse themselves in the vibrant atmosphere of Sorrento's community life.

Visitor centers and tourist assistance services play a crucial role in enhancing the travel experience for visitors to Sorrento. By providing valuable information, personalized recommendations, and support services, these centers help travelers navigate the town with ease, discover hidden gems, and create unforgettable memories during their stay. Whether you're seeking guidance on accommodations, planning customized itineraries, or experiencing local culture, tourist assistants are there to ensure that your visit to Sorrento is memorable and enjoyable.

CHAPTER 6
CULINARY DELIGHTS

6.1. Traditional Italian and Sorrentine Cuisine

Sorrento, with its stunning vistas of the Bay of Naples and Mount Vesuvius, is not only a feast for the eyes but also a haven for food enthusiasts. Nestled in the Campania region of Italy, Sorrento boasts a rich culinary heritage that blends traditional Italian flavors with unique Sorrentine twists. From fresh seafood to delectable pastries, Sorrento offers a tantalizing array of dishes that reflect its cultural heritage and coastal bounty.

Pizza Margherita: A Taste of Italian Tradition

One cannot discuss Italian cuisine without mentioning pizza, and Sorrento is no exception. The birthplace of pizza, Naples, lies just a stone's throw away, and Sorrento's pizzerias uphold this tradition with pride. Among the plethora of pizzas available, the Pizza Margherita stands out as a timeless classic. Topped with tomatoes, mozzarella cheese, fresh basil, and a drizzle of olive oil, this simple yet flavorful pizza is a must-try for visitors. One can find authentic Pizza Margheritas at pizzerias throughout Sorrento, with prices typically ranging from €8 to €15 depending on the establishment and size. For an authentic experience, head to Pizzeria Da Franco located on Via degli Aranci, or try Pizzeria Aurora on Piazza Tasso. Both establishments offer cozy atmospheres and mouthwatering pizzas that will satisfy any craving.

Insalata Caprese: A Refreshing Antipasto

Another iconic dish originating from the Campania region is the Insalata Caprese. This simple yet elegant salad features ripe tomatoes, creamy buffalo mozzarella, fresh basil leaves, and a drizzle of extra virgin olive oil. The vibrant colors and contrasting flavors make it a perfect starter or light lunch option, especially on warm summer days. Visitors can expect to pay around €8 to €12 for a serving of Insalata Caprese at most restaurants and trattorias in Sorrento. For a delightful dining experience with a view, head to Ristorante Il Buco located near Marina Grande. Situated right by the sea, this charming restaurant offers excellent Insalata Caprese alongside panoramic views of the bay.

Gnocchi alla Sorrentina: Comfort Food with a Local Twist

Gnocchi alla Sorrentina is a hearty pasta dish that exemplifies the marriage of Italian and Sorrentine culinary traditions. Soft potato dumplings are smothered in a rich tomato sauce, flavored with fresh basil and melted mozzarella cheese. This indulgent dish is a favorite among locals and visitors alike, offering a comforting taste of Sorrento's culinary heritage. Prices for Gnocchi alla Sorrentina typically range from €10 to €18 depending on the restaurant and portion size. For an authentic rendition of this Sorrentine specialty, visit Ristorante Tasso located in the heart of Sorrento's historic center. With its cozy ambiance and attentive service, it's the perfect spot to savor this classic dish.

Limoncello: Sorrento's Signature Digestif

No visit to Sorrento would be complete without sampling its famous Limoncello liqueur. Made from the zest of Sorrento lemons, alcohol, water, and sugar, Limoncello is a sweet and tangy digestif that perfectly encapsulates the flavors of the region. Visitors can enjoy Limoncello on its own as a post-meal treat or use it to elevate desserts such as gelato or cake. Prices for a bottle of Limoncello vary depending on the quality and size, with souvenir-sized bottles starting from €10 and larger bottles ranging from €15 to €2 For a wide selection of Limoncello varieties and other local liqueurs, visit Limonoro located on Corso Italia. This charming shop offers tastings and knowledgeable staff who can help you find the perfect bottle to take home as a memento of your Sorrento experience.

Sfogliatella: A Sweet Conclusion

To round off a meal in Sorrento, indulge in a Sfogliatella, a traditional pastry that hails from the nearby city of Naples. This flaky, shell-shaped treat is filled with a sweet ricotta and citrus filling, creating a delightful contrast of textures and flavors. Whether enjoyed with a cup of espresso or savored on its own, Sfogliatella is the perfect way to satisfy your sweet tooth. Prices for Sfogliatella typically range from €1.50 to €3 per pastry, making it an affordable indulgence for visitors. For the best Sfogliatella in Sorrento, head to Pasticceria Andrea Pansa located on Via San Cesareo. This historic pastry shop has been delighting locals and visitors alike since 1830 with its freshly baked treats and charming ambiance.

Sorrento's culinary scene offers a delightful blend of traditional Italian dishes and Sorrentine specialties that are sure to tantalize the taste buds of visitors. From classic pizzas to indulgent pastries, there's something for everyone to enjoy in this picturesque coastal town. So, come hungry and immerse yourself in the flavors of Sorrento – a culinary journey you won't soon forget!

6.2. Seafood Restaurants and Pizzerias

Sorrento, with its breathtaking coastal views and rich culinary heritage, is a haven for seafood lovers and pizza enthusiasts alike. Nestled along the stunning Amalfi Coast in the Campania region of Italy, Sorrento boasts an abundance of seafood restaurants and pizzerias that showcase the freshest local ingredients and traditional flavors. From succulent seafood dishes to mouthwatering pizzas, visitors to Sorrento are spoiled for choice when it comes to dining options.

Savoring the Freshest Catch: Seafood Restaurants

Sorrento's proximity to the Mediterranean Sea makes it an ideal destination for sampling freshly caught seafood delicacies. The town's seafood restaurants pride themselves on sourcing the finest local ingredients and preparing them with skill and passion. Visitors can expect to indulge in an array of seafood dishes, from grilled fish to seafood pasta, all bursting with the flavors of the sea.

Ristorante Il Buco: A Seafood Oasis

Located near Marina Grande, Ristorante Il Buco offers a quintessential seafood dining experience with panoramic views of the bay. Guests can dine al fresco on the terrace while enjoying dishes such as Linguine alle Vongole (clam linguine) and Grilled Octopus. Prices at Ristorante Il Buco typically range from €20 to €40 per dish, reflecting the quality of the ingredients and the picturesque setting. Reservations are recommended, especially during the peak tourist season, to secure a table with a view.

Trattoria Da Emilia: A Family-owned Gem

For a more intimate dining experience, visitors can head to Trattoria Da Emilia, a charming family-owned restaurant tucked away in Sorrento's historic center. Known for its warm hospitality and authentic Sorrentine cuisine, Trattoria Da Emilia serves up classic seafood dishes such as Spaghetti ai Frutti di Mare (seafood spaghetti) and Pesce alla Griglia (grilled fish). Prices at this trattoria are more budget-friendly, ranging from €15 to €25 per dish, making it a popular choice among locals and tourists alike. When dining at seafood restaurants in Sorrento, it's essential to inquire about the day's specials, as many establishments feature seasonal dishes showcasing the freshest catch. Additionally, be sure to pair your meal with a crisp local white wine, such as Greco di Tufo or Falanghina, to enhance the flavors of the seafood. Reservations are recommended, especially for waterfront restaurants, to secure the best seats and avoid long wait times during peak dining hours.

Indulging in Pizza Perfection: Pizzerias in Sorrento

No visit to Sorrento would be complete without savoring a slice of authentic Neapolitan pizza, and the town boasts an array of pizzerias that uphold this culinary tradition with pride. From wood-fired ovens to handcrafted dough, Sorrento's pizzerias are dedicated to delivering pizza perfection to every hungry patron.

Pizzeria Da Franco: A Slice of Tradition

Situated on Via degli Aranci, Pizzeria Da Franco is a local favorite known for its crispy yet chewy crust and generous toppings. Visitors can choose from an array of classic pizzas, including Margherita, Marinara, and Quattro Stagioni, all prepared with the freshest ingredients. Prices at Pizzeria Da Franco range from €8 to €15 per pizza, depending on the size and toppings chosen. The cozy atmosphere and friendly service make it an excellent choice for families and groups.

Pizzeria Aurora: Pizza with a View

For a pizza experience with a view, visitors can head to Pizzeria Aurora located on Piazza Tasso. Situated in the heart of Sorrento's bustling town center, Pizzeria Aurora offers diners the chance to enjoy their pizza while soaking in the sights and sounds of the lively piazza. The menu features an extensive selection of pizzas, including vegetarian and seafood options, with prices ranging from €10 to €18 per pizza. Reservations are recommended, especially for outdoor seating, to secure a table with a view. When dining at pizzerias in Sorrento, be sure to try the local specialty, Pizza

Margherita, for a taste of authentic Neapolitan cuisine. Additionally, don't be afraid to ask for recommendations from the staff, as they are often knowledgeable about the best pizza toppings and flavor combinations. For the full experience, pair your pizza with a refreshing local beer or a glass of Limoncello for a sweet finish to your meal.

Sorrento's seafood restaurants and pizzerias offer visitors a culinary journey through the flavors of the Amalfi Coast and the traditions of Neapolitan cuisine. Whether indulging in fresh seafood by the waterfront or savoring a slice of pizza in the town center, dining in Sorrento is sure to be a memorable experience for food enthusiasts of all tastes. So, come hungry and embark on a gastronomic adventure through the streets of Sorrento – where every meal is a celebration of Italian culinary heritage.

6.3. Cafes and Gelaterias

Sorrento, with its charming streets and stunning coastal views, offers not only a feast for the eyes but also a paradise for those with a sweet tooth. From aromatic espresso to creamy gelato, the town is dotted with cafes and gelaterias that beckon visitors to indulge in delightful treats. Steeped in Italian coffee culture and renowned for its artisanal gelato, Sorrento's cafes and gelaterias are an essential part of the town's culinary experience.

Savoring the Essence of Italian Coffee Culture: Cafes in Sorrento

Cafes in Sorrento are more than just places to grab a quick caffeine fix – they are institutions that embody the essence of Italian coffee culture. Visitors can expect to sip on expertly brewed espresso or linger over a frothy cappuccino while soaking in the ambiance of Sorrento's bustling streets.

Cafe Latino: A Taste of Tradition

Nestled in the heart of Sorrento's historic center, Cafe Latino exudes old-world charm with its vintage decor and welcoming atmosphere. Here, visitors can enjoy a traditional Italian breakfast of espresso and cornetto (croissant) or opt for a refreshing caffe freddo (iced coffee) on warm summer days. Prices at Cafe Latino are reasonable, with espresso starting at €1.50 and specialty drinks such as cappuccino or caffe latte ranging from €2.50 to €4.

Pasticceria Bar Fiorentino: A Sweet Haven

For those with a penchant for pastries, Pasticceria Bar Fiorentino is a must-visit destination in Sorrento. This beloved cafe boasts a mouthwatering selection of freshly baked treats, including cannoli, sfogliatelle, and creamy tiramisu. Visitors can pair their pastries with a fragrant espresso or indulge in a decadent hot chocolate topped with whipped cream. Prices at Pasticceria Bar Fiorentino are affordable, with pastries starting at €1.50 and coffee drinks ranging from €2 to €4. To fully immerse yourself in the Italian cafe experience, take the time to savor your coffee slowly and enjoy the lively atmosphere around you. Many cafes in Sorrento offer outdoor seating, providing the perfect opportunity for people-watching while you sip your drink. Additionally, don't hesitate to strike up a conversation with the barista or locals – Italians are known for their warmth and hospitality, and you may just make a new friend over a cup of coffee.

Indulging in Gelato Delights: Gelaterias in Sorrento

No visit to Sorrento would be complete without indulging in a scoop or two of gelato, and the town boasts an array of gelaterias that churn out creamy delights in a rainbow of flavors. Made with fresh, locally sourced ingredients, Sorrento's gelato is a true culinary delight that captures the essence of Italian craftsmanship.

Raki: Gelato Artigianale: A Gelato Gem

Located near Piazza Tasso, Raki: Gelato Artigianale is a hidden gem beloved by locals and visitors alike. This artisanal gelateria prides itself on using only the finest ingredients to create gelato that is bursting with flavor and freshness. With an ever-changing menu featuring seasonal fruits and inventive combinations, Raki offers a gelato experience like no other. Prices at Raki: Gelato Artigianale are reasonable, with a small cone or cup starting at €2.50 and larger sizes ranging from €3.50 to €5.

Gelateria David: A Family Tradition

For a taste of tradition, visitors can head to Gelateria David, a family-owned gelateria that has been delighting customers for generations. Located on Corso Italia, Gelateria David offers a wide selection of classic gelato flavors, from rich chocolate to tangy lemon, all made with love and care. Prices at Gelateria David are affordable, with a small cone or cup starting at €2.50 and larger sizes ranging from €3.50 to €5. When choosing a gelateria in Sorrento, look for establishments that display their gelato in covered containers to ensure freshness and hygiene. Additionally, don't be afraid to sample multiple flavors before making your selection – many gelaterias allow customers to try before they buy. And remember, gelato is best enjoyed slowly, so take your time to savor each spoonful and appreciate the artistry that goes into crafting this beloved Italian treat. Sorrento's cafes and gelaterias offer visitors a delectable journey through the flavors of Italy, from aromatic espresso to creamy gelato. Whether sipping on coffee in a quaint cafe or indulging in gelato on a sunny afternoon, dining in Sorrento is sure to be a memorable experience for food enthusiasts of all tastes. So, come hungry and embark on a culinary adventure through the streets of Sorrento – where every bite is a celebration of Italian craftsmanship and tradition.

6.4. Local Wine and Limoncello Tasting

Sorrento, with its stunning coastal vistas and rich cultural heritage, offers visitors a taste of Italy's liquid delights through its local wine and Limoncello. Nestled in the Campania region, Sorrento boasts a vibrant wine scene, with vineyards producing a variety of wines that reflect the terroir of the area. Additionally, the town is famous for its Limoncello liqueur, made from the fragrant lemons that thrive in the region's sunny climate. Embarking on a wine and Limoncello tasting journey in Sorrento is not just a culinary experience but also an opportunity to immerse oneself in the flavors and traditions of southern Italy.

Sorrento's Vinicultural Heritage: Local Wine Tasting

Sorrento's vinicultural heritage dates back centuries, with the region's volcanic soil and Mediterranean climate providing ideal conditions for grape cultivation. Visitors to Sorrento have the opportunity to sample a diverse selection of wines, from crisp whites to full-bodied reds, all crafted with care by local winemakers.

Cantine Marisa Cuomo: A Winemaking Marvel

One of the most renowned wineries in Sorrento is Cantine Marisa Cuomo, located in the picturesque town of Furore along the Amalfi Coast. Perched on steep terraced slopes overlooking the sea, this award-winning winery produces a range of exceptional wines, including the signature Fiorduva and Furore Bianco. Visitors can embark on guided tours of the vineyards and cellars, followed by tastings of Cantine Marisa Cuomo's exquisite wines. Prices for wine tastings at Cantine Marisa Cuomo vary depending on the tour package, with options starting from €20 per person. When visiting wineries in Sorrento, it's advisable to book tastings in advance, especially during the peak tourist season, to secure a spot. Additionally, don't hesitate to ask questions about the winemaking process and the characteristics of each wine – the staff at the wineries are usually passionate about their craft and happy to share their knowledge with visitors.

Savoring Sorrento's Liquid Sunshine: Limoncello Tasting

No visit to Sorrento would be complete without sampling its signature liqueur, Limoncello. Made from the zest of Sorrento lemons, alcohol, water, and sugar, Limoncello is a sweet and tangy digestif that captures the essence of the Amalfi Coast's sunny climate. Visitors to Sorrento can indulge in Limoncello tastings at local shops and distilleries, where they can sample different varieties and learn about the traditional production methods.

Limonoro: A Limoncello Wonderland

Limonoro is one of Sorrento's most renowned Limoncello producers, offering visitors the chance to sample a wide range of Limoncello varieties and other citrus liqueurs. Located on Corso Italia, Limonoro welcomes guests with its vibrant yellow storefront and inviting aroma of citrus. Visitors can enjoy guided tastings led by knowledgeable staff who provide insights into the history and production of Limoncello. Prices for Limoncello tastings at Limonoro typically range from €5 to €10 per person, depending on the number of samples. When sampling Limoncello in Sorrento, be sure to pace yourself and drink responsibly, as the liqueur can be quite potent. Additionally, consider purchasing a bottle of your favorite Limoncello to take home as a souvenir – many shops offer beautifully packaged bottles that make for perfect gifts or mementos of your time in Sorrento.

Combining Wine and Limoncello Tasting Experiences

For those looking to experience the best of both worlds, several establishments in Sorrento offer combined wine and Limoncello tastings, allowing visitors to sample the region's liquid delights in one immersive experience. These tastings often include a selection of local wines paired with Limoncello or other citrus liqueurs, providing a comprehensive overview of Sorrento's culinary heritage.

Sorrento's wine and Limoncello tasting experiences offer visitors a unique opportunity to explore the flavors and traditions of southern Italy. Whether sampling award-winning wines at vineyards overlooking the sea or indulging in tangy Limoncello at local shops, visitors to Sorrento are sure to delight in the region's liquid delights. So, come raise a glass and toast to the vibrant flavors of Sorrento – where every sip is a celebration of Italian craftsmanship and tradition.

6.5. Cooking Classes and Culinary Tours

Sorrento, with its rich culinary heritage and vibrant food scene, offers visitors the opportunity to delve deeper into Italian cuisine through cooking classes and culinary tours. Nestled along the stunning Amalfi Coast in the Campania region of Italy, Sorrento is renowned for its fresh seafood, fragrant lemons, and artisanal ingredients – making it the perfect destination for food enthusiasts eager to learn the secrets of Italian cooking. From hands-on cooking experiences to guided tours of local markets and vineyards, Sorrento's cooking classes and culinary tours promise to satisfy both the palate and the soul.

Unlocking the Secrets of Italian Cuisine: Cooking Classes

Cooking classes in Sorrento provide visitors with the chance to roll up their sleeves and learn to create authentic Italian dishes under the guidance of expert chefs. From mastering the art of pasta-making to perfecting the balance of flavors in traditional sauces, participants can immerse themselves in the culinary traditions of southern Italy while honing their cooking skills.

Ciao Laura Culinary Vacation: A Taste of Tradition

Ciao Laura Culinary Vacation offers immersive cooking experiences led by acclaimed chef Laura and her team of culinary experts. Located in a charming villa overlooking the Bay of Naples, participants can choose from a variety of cooking classes focusing on regional specialties such as Neapolitan pizza, handmade pasta, and fresh seafood dishes. Prices for cooking classes at Ciao Laura Culinary Vacation vary depending on the duration and inclusions, with half-day classes starting from €100 per person and full-day experiences ranging from €150 to €200 per person.

Cooking with Nonna: A Family Affair

For those seeking a more intimate cooking experience, Cooking with Nonna offers personalized classes led by Nonna Rosa, a local grandmother with a passion for sharing her culinary traditions. Participants join Nonna Rosa in her home kitchen to learn the secrets of traditional Sorrentine recipes passed down through generations. Prices for cooking classes with Nonna Rosa start from €80 per person for a half-day experience and €150 per person for a full-day immersion. When booking cooking classes in Sorrento, it's essential to inquire about the class size and level of hands-on participation to ensure that it aligns with your preferences and skill level. Additionally, be sure to notify the organizers of any dietary restrictions or food allergies in advance, so they can accommodate your needs. Most cooking classes include a meal or tasting session where participants can enjoy the fruits of their labor, so arrive hungry and ready to feast on your culinary creations.

Exploring Sorrento's Culinary Landscape: Culinary Tours

Culinary tours in Sorrento offer visitors the opportunity to explore the town's bustling markets, artisanal shops, and local eateries while gaining insights into the region's gastronomic traditions. Led by knowledgeable guides, these tours provide a behind-the-scenes look at Sorrento's vibrant food scene and the people who shape it.

Sorrento Food Tour: A Gastronomic Journey

Sorrento Food Tour offers guided culinary tours that take participants on a journey through the town's hidden gems and culinary hotspots. From bustling markets brimming with fresh produce to quaint cafes serving authentic Italian pastries, participants can sample a diverse array of Sorrento's culinary delights. Prices for Sorrento Food Tour vary depending on the duration and inclusions, with half-day tours starting from €50 per person and full-day experiences ranging from €80 to €100 per person.

Sorrento Wine Tasting Tour: A Toast to Tradition

For wine enthusiasts, Sorrento Wine Tasting Tour offers guided excursions to local vineyards and wineries, where participants can sample a selection of wines paired with artisanal cheeses and cured meats. Led by sommeliers and wine experts, these tours provide insights into the region's winemaking traditions and terroir. Prices for Sorrento

Wine Tasting Tour vary depending on the duration and inclusions, with half-day tours starting from €60 per person and full-day experiences ranging from €100 to €150 per person. When joining culinary tours in Sorrento, wear comfortable shoes and clothing suitable for walking and exploring outdoor markets and shops. Be prepared to sample a variety of foods and beverages throughout the tour, so pace yourself to avoid overindulging. Additionally, don't forget to bring a camera to capture the sights, sounds, and flavors of Sorrento's vibrant culinary landscape.

Cooking classes and culinary tours in Sorrento offer visitors the chance to immerse themselves in the region's rich gastronomic traditions while honing their cooking skills and exploring local markets and eateries. Whether learning to make pasta from scratch or sampling wines at a local vineyard, participants are sure to come away with a deeper appreciation for Italian cuisine and the people who create it. So, come hungry and curious, and embark on a culinary adventure through the streets of Sorrento – where every dish tells a story of tradition, passion, and flavor.

CHAPTER 7
CULTURE AND HERITAGE

7.1. Historical Buildings and Architecture

Situated along the rugged coastline of the Sorrentine Peninsula, Sorrento boasts a rich tapestry of historical buildings and architectural treasures that speak to its storied past. From ancient Roman ruins to medieval churches and grand palaces, the town's architectural landscape is a testament to its cultural heritage and significance. Exploring Sorrento's historical buildings offers visitors a glimpse into the town's fascinating history and provides an opportunity to marvel at its architectural splendor.

Duomo di Sorrento: A Spiritual Centerpiece

Located in the heart of Sorrento's historic center, the Duomo di Sorrento, or Sorrento Cathedral, is a prominent landmark that dates back to the 15th century. This Baroque-style cathedral is dedicated to Saints Philip and James and features a stunning facade adorned with intricate marble carvings and a bell tower that offers panoramic views of the town. Visitors can explore the cathedral's interior, which houses notable works of art, including a magnificent wooden crucifix and a 13th-century Byzantine icon of the Madonna. Entry to the Duomo di Sorrento is free, making it an accessible and enriching cultural experience for visitors of all ages.

Chiostro di San Francesco: Tranquility Amidst History

Adjacent to the Duomo di Sorrento lies the Chiostro di San Francesco, or Cloister of San Francesco, a serene oasis of tranquility amidst the bustling streets of Sorrento. Dating back to the 14th century, this cloister features a beautiful garden surrounded by porticoes adorned with ancient frescoes and marble columns. Visitors can wander through the cloister, admiring its architectural details and soaking in the peaceful atmosphere. Entry to the Chiostro di San Francesco is typically included with admission to the Duomo di Sorrento, making it a convenient stop for those exploring the historic center.

Villa Comunale: Gardens with a View

Perched on a cliff overlooking the Bay of Naples, Villa Comunale is a picturesque park that offers panoramic views of the sea and Mount Vesuvius. Originally the site of a Roman villa, the park was transformed into a public garden in the 19th century and features lush greenery, colorful flower beds, and winding pathways. Visitors can stroll through the gardens, stopping to admire the ornate fountain and statues scattered throughout. The highlight of Villa Comunale is its belvedere, or viewpoint, which offers breathtaking vistas of the coastline and is the perfect spot for capturing memorable photographs. Entry to Villa Comunale is free, making it an ideal destination for a leisurely stroll or a relaxing picnic with a view.

Basilica di Sant'Antonino: Patron Saint of Sorrento

Dedicated to Saint Anthony of Padua, the Basilica di Sant'Antonino is a striking example of Neoclassical architecture that dominates the skyline of Sorrento's historic center. Built in the 11th century atop the ruins of a Roman temple, the basilica houses the relics of Saint Antonino, the patron saint of Sorrento. Visitors can admire the basilica's elegant facade and impressive dome, as well as its ornate interior adorned with marble altars and frescoes depicting scenes from the saint's life. Entry to the Basilica di Sant'Antonino is free, and visitors are welcome to attend Mass or simply explore the sanctuary's rich history and spiritual significance.

Correale di Terranova Museum: A Palatial Treasure Trove

Situated in a grand palazzo overlooking the Bay of Naples, the Correale di Terranova Museum is home to an extensive collection of art, artifacts, and archaeological finds that offer insight into Sorrento's cultural heritage. Founded in the 19th century by the Correale family, the museum's eclectic exhibits include Renaissance paintings, ancient Roman sculptures, and decorative arts from the Neapolitan Baroque period. Visitors can wander through the palazzo's opulent rooms, admiring its frescoed ceilings, gilded furnishings, and panoramic views of the coastline. Entry to the Correale di Terranova Museum is €8 for adults and €5 for students, with discounts available for groups and guided tours.

Valle dei Mulini: A Glimpse into Sorrento's Industrial Past

Tucked away in the heart of Sorrento's historic center lies Valle dei Mulini, or the Valley of the Mills, a hidden gem that offers a glimpse into the town's industrial past. Dating back to the 10th century, this secluded ravine is home to the ruins of ancient flour mills and sawmills that once powered Sorrento's thriving economy. Visitors can descend into the valley via a series of steps, exploring the atmospheric ruins and marveling at the ingenuity of past generations. Entry to Valle dei Mulini is free, and the site is accessible year-round, providing a fascinating glimpse into Sorrento's lesser-known history.

Exploring Sorrento's historical buildings and architecture offers visitors a captivating journey through the town's rich cultural heritage and storied past. From majestic cathedrals to serene cloisters and opulent palazzos, each architectural gem tells a story of centuries-old traditions and the enduring legacy of Sorrento's inhabitants. Whether admiring ancient frescoes, savoring panoramic views, or delving into the town's industrial history, Sorrento's historical buildings beckon visitors to embark on a voyage of discovery and exploration. So, come wander through the streets of Sorrento and uncover the secrets of its architectural treasures – where every corner reveals a piece of history waiting to be explored.

7.2. Music and Performing Arts

Sorrento, with its enchanting coastal setting and vibrant cultural scene, offers visitors a rich tapestry of music and performing arts that reflect its historical and cultural heritage. From traditional Neapolitan songs to classical concerts and theatrical performances, Sorrento's music and performing arts scene provide a captivating glimpse into the town's artistic soul. Whether attending a concert in a historic theater or enjoying a street performance along the bustling promenade, visitors to Sorrento are sure to be enthralled by the sights and sounds of its musical traditions.

Teatro Tasso: A Cultural Gem

Located in the heart of Sorrento's historic center, Teatro Tasso is a cultural hub that showcases a diverse array of music and performing arts events throughout the year. Dating back to the 19th century, this elegant theater features a stunning neoclassical facade and a beautifully appointed interior with plush seating and ornate decorations. Visitors can attend a variety of performances at Teatro Tasso, including classical concerts, opera productions, and theatrical plays. Entry fees for events at Teatro Tasso vary depending on the performance and seating category, with tickets typically available for purchase online or at the box office.

Correale Music Festival: A Symphony by the Sea

Every summer, Sorrento comes alive with the sounds of the Correale Music Festival, a prestigious event that attracts world-class musicians and performers to the town's stunning waterfront. Held at the Correale di Terranova Museum, the festival features a series of concerts and recitals showcasing a diverse repertoire of classical music, opera, and chamber music. Visitors can enjoy performances by renowned orchestras, soloists, and ensembles against the backdrop of the Bay of Naples and Mount Vesuvius. Tickets for the Correale Music Festival can be purchased online or at the museum's box office, with prices varying depending on the performance and seating availability.

Sorrento Musical: A Theatrical Extravaganza

For a taste of Sorrento's theatrical heritage, visitors can attend a performance of Sorrento Musical, a lively show that celebrates the town's history, culture, and traditions through music and dance. Held at various venues throughout Sorrento, including Teatro Tasso and outdoor amphitheaters, Sorrento Musical features a talented cast of performers who bring to life the stories and characters that define the town's identity. From traditional folk songs to modern pop hits, the musical showcases the diversity and vibrancy of Sorrento's musical landscape. Tickets for Sorrento Musical can be purchased online or at designated ticket outlets in the town center, with prices ranging from €20 to €50 depending on the seating category and performance date.

Street Performances: Music in the Open Air

One of the highlights of visiting Sorrento is experiencing the spontaneous street performances that enliven the town's bustling streets and piazzas. From talented musicians playing traditional Italian melodies to energetic dance troupes performing lively routines, street performers add a sense of excitement and charm to Sorrento's vibrant atmosphere. Visitors can stroll along the promenade or wander through the narrow alleyways of the historic center, stopping to enjoy impromptu performances that capture the spirit of Sorrento's musical traditions. Entry to street performances is free, making them accessible to all visitors who happen upon them during their explorations of the town.

Sorrento Jazz Festival: A Celebration of Jazz

For jazz enthusiasts, the Sorrento Jazz Festival is a must-visit event that brings together top jazz musicians from around the world for a week of unforgettable performances. Held at various venues throughout Sorrento, including theaters, clubs, and outdoor stages, the festival features a diverse lineup of jazz styles and genres, ranging from classic standards to contemporary fusion. Visitors can immerse themselves in the world of jazz, attending concerts, workshops, and jam sessions that showcase the creativity and talent of the participating artists. Tickets for the Sorrento Jazz Festival can be purchased online or at designated ticket outlets in the town center, with prices varying depending on the venue and performance.

Traditional Folk Performances: Preserving Cultural Heritage

Sorrento's musical and performing arts scene also includes traditional folk performances that pay homage to the town's rich cultural heritage. From Tarantella dance troupes to folk music ensembles, these performances celebrate the customs and traditions of Sorrento's inhabitants, passing down ancient songs and dances from generation to generation. Visitors can attend folk performances at local festivals, cultural events, and traditional celebrations throughout the year, gaining insight into the unique rhythms and melodies that define Sorrento's musical identity. Entry to traditional folk performances is often free or involves a nominal fee, making them accessible to all visitors who wish to experience Sorrento's cultural heritage.

Sorrento's music and performing arts scene offers visitors a captivating journey through the town's historical and cultural landscape. Whether attending a concert at Teatro Tasso, enjoying a street performance along the promenade, or immersing oneself in the sounds of the Correale Music Festival, visitors to Sorrento are sure to be enchanted by the town's musical traditions and artistic vibrancy. So, come experience the magic of

Sorrento's music and performing arts – where every note and every step tells a story of creativity, passion, and cultural heritage.

7.3. Festivals and Cultural Events

Sorrento is not only renowned for its breathtaking landscapes but also for its vibrant festivals and cultural events that captivate visitors year-round. From traditional religious celebrations to lively music festivals and colorful processions, Sorrento's cultural calendar is brimming with events that showcase the town's rich history, heritage, and community spirit. Attending these festivals offers visitors a unique opportunity to immerse themselves in Sorrento's cultural tapestry and experience the warmth and hospitality of its inhabitants.

Lemon Festival: A Citrus Extravaganza

One of Sorrento's most iconic events is the Lemon Festival, held annually in the spring to celebrate the town's prized citrus fruit – the Sorrento lemon. Located in the historic center of Sorrento, the Lemon Festival features elaborate displays of lemon-themed artwork, sculptures, and decorations that adorn the streets and piazzas. Visitors can marvel at the creativity and craftsmanship on display, as local artisans showcase their talents through intricate lemon carvings and installations. The festival also includes live music performances, street food vendors offering lemon-inspired delicacies, and cultural activities that highlight the importance of lemons in Sorrento's culinary and agricultural traditions. Entry to the Lemon Festival is typically free, making it accessible to all visitors who wish to experience the zest and vibrancy of Sorrento's citrus culture.

Sorrento Summer Festival: Music under the Stars

During the summer months, Sorrento comes alive with the sounds of the Sorrento Summer Festival, a series of outdoor concerts and performances held in scenic venues throughout the town. From classical music to pop, rock, and jazz, the festival features a diverse lineup of national and international artists who entertain audiences under the starry Mediterranean sky. Visitors can enjoy performances at historic sites such as Villa

Comunale, Piazza Tasso, and the Marina Grande waterfront, soaking in the ambiance and atmosphere of Sorrento's summer nights. Tickets for the Sorrento Summer Festival can be purchased online or at designated ticket outlets, with prices varying depending on the artist and venue.

Sorrento Film Festival: A Cinematic Celebration

Film enthusiasts flock to Sorrento each year for the Sorrento Film Festival, a prestigious event that celebrates the art of cinema and showcases a selection of independent films, documentaries, and shorts from around the world. Held at various theaters and screening venues in Sorrento's historic center, the festival provides a platform for emerging filmmakers to showcase their work and engage with audiences. Visitors can attend film screenings, panel discussions, and Q&A sessions with filmmakers, gaining insights into the creative process and the stories behind the films. Entry fees for the Sorrento Film Festival vary depending on the type of pass or ticket package purchased, with discounts available for students and festival pass holders.

Sorrento Easter Celebrations: A Time of Tradition and Reflection

Easter holds special significance in Sorrento, with the town's residents coming together to observe religious traditions and celebrate the resurrection of Jesus Christ. The Easter celebrations in Sorrento are marked by solemn processions, religious rituals, and festive gatherings that reflect the town's deeply rooted Catholic heritage. Visitors can witness the stirring processions of the Mysteries of Sorrento, where statues depicting scenes from the Passion of Christ are paraded through the streets amidst prayers and hymns. Churches throughout Sorrento hold special Masses and religious services, inviting visitors to participate in the spiritual journey of Easter. Entry to Easter celebrations in Sorrento is free, and visitors are welcome to observe and participate in the religious rituals and cultural traditions of the season.

Sorrento Wine Festival: A Toast to Local Flavors

Wine aficionados and food enthusiasts converge on Sorrento each fall for the Sorrento Wine Festival, a gastronomic celebration that highlights the region's rich culinary heritage and wine-making traditions. Held in the historic center of Sorrento, the festival features tastings of locally produced wines, olive oils, cheeses, and other gourmet specialties from Campania and beyond. Visitors can sample a variety of wines from renowned vineyards and wineries, learning about the terroir and production methods that give each vintage its unique flavor profile. The Sorrento Wine Festival also includes cooking demonstrations, wine pairing workshops, and live music performances that add to the festive atmosphere. Entry to the Sorrento Wine Festival is typically free, with tasting tickets available for purchase at the event.

Christmas Markets and Nativity Scenes: A Season of Joy

The holiday season in Sorrento is a magical time filled with festive markets, twinkling lights, and traditional nativity scenes that evoke the spirit of Christmas. Visitors can stroll through the streets of Sorrento's historic center, browsing stalls selling handmade crafts, gifts, and holiday treats at the Christmas markets. The town's churches and piazzas are adorned with elaborate nativity scenes, or presepi, depicting the biblical story of the birth of Jesus Christ. Visitors can admire these intricate displays and marvel at the craftsmanship of local artisans who create them. The Christmas season in Sorrento also includes concerts, carolers, and other festive events that bring joy and cheer to residents and visitors alike. Entry to Christmas markets and nativity scenes in Sorrento is typically free, making it a delightful destination for holiday shoppers and sightseers.

Sorrento's festivals and cultural events offer visitors a captivating glimpse into the town's rich history, traditions, and community spirit. Whether attending the Lemon Festival, soaking in the sounds of the Sorrento Summer Festival, or experiencing the solemnity of Easter celebrations, visitors to Sorrento are sure to be enchanted by the town's vibrant cultural scene. So, come join in the festivities and celebrations – where every event is a celebration of Sorrento's unique charm and cultural heritage.

7.4. Crafts and Local Artisans

From intricate inlaid woodwork to hand-painted ceramics and delicate lacework, Sorrento's crafts and artisanal products reflect the town's cultural heritage and the skill and creativity of its local artisans. Exploring Sorrento's craft workshops and boutiques offers visitors a unique opportunity to discover one-of-a-kind souvenirs and immerse themselves in the town's artisanal traditions.

Wood Inlay: A Time-Honored Craft

Sorrento is famous for its exquisite wood inlay, or intarsia, which dates back to the 18th century and remains a hallmark of the town's craftsmanship. Located in the historic center of Sorrento, visitors can find numerous workshops and boutiques where skilled artisans create intricate designs using various types of wood, including walnut, cherry, and olive. The art of wood inlay involves painstakingly cutting and assembling pieces of wood to form intricate patterns and images, resulting in stunning works of art that adorn furniture, jewelry boxes, and decorative items. Visitors can watch artisans at work in their workshops, witnessing the intricate process of wood inlay and perhaps even trying their hand at creating their own masterpiece. Entry to wood inlay workshops is typically free, with the option to purchase handmade souvenirs and gifts.

Ceramics: Beauty in Every Brushstroke

Another cherished craft in Sorrento is ceramic pottery, which has been practiced for centuries and continues to thrive in the town's bustling workshops and studios. Located in the historic center and along the scenic coastal roads, visitors can explore pottery studios and boutiques where artisans create hand-painted ceramics inspired by the vibrant colors and motifs of the Amalfi Coast. From decorative tiles and tableware to figurines and vases, Sorrento's ceramic artisans showcase their talents through a diverse array of products that capture the beauty and essence of the region. Visitors can observe artisans painting and glazing ceramics, learning about the traditional techniques and designs that have been passed down through generations. Entry to ceramic workshops is often free, with the option to purchase handmade ceramics as souvenirs or gifts.

Lacework: Delicate Artistry

Sorrento is also renowned for its delicate lacework, which has been a cherished tradition in the town for centuries. Located in the historic center and along quaint alleyways, visitors can find lace shops and boutiques where skilled artisans create intricate lace patterns using fine threads and delicate needles. Sorrentine lacework, known as merletto, is characterized by its intricate designs and meticulous craftsmanship, with motifs inspired by nature, mythology, and local folklore. Visitors can watch artisans at work in their studios, marveling at the precision and skill required to create such delicate lacework. Entry to lacework studios is typically free, with the option to purchase handmade lace products as souvenirs or gifts.

Artisanal Leather Goods: Italian Elegance

For lovers of fine leather goods, Sorrento offers a wealth of artisanal boutiques and workshops where skilled craftsmen create high-quality leather products using traditional techniques. Located in the historic center and along the main shopping streets, visitors can find leather shops specializing in handcrafted belts, bags, wallets, and accessories made from the finest Italian leather. Sorrento's leather artisans take pride in their workmanship, combining centuries-old techniques with modern design to create timeless pieces that embody Italian elegance and style. Visitors can browse leather boutiques, watch artisans at work in their workshops, and even commission custom-made leather goods tailored to their preferences. Entry to leather workshops is typically free, with the option to purchase handmade leather products as souvenirs or gifts.

Artisanal Food Products: Gastronomic Treasures

In addition to crafts, Sorrento is also known for its artisanal food products that showcase the region's culinary heritage and local ingredients. Visitors can explore markets and specialty shops in the historic center and along the waterfront, where they can find an array of gourmet delights such as olive oil, limoncello, liqueurs, jams, and preserves. Sorrento's artisanal food producers take pride in using traditional methods and locally sourced ingredients to create authentic flavors that reflect the essence of the Amalfi Coast. Visitors can sample and purchase artisanal food products, learning about the production process and the cultural significance of each delicacy. Entry to food markets and shops is typically free, with the option to purchase gourmet products to enjoy during their stay or to take home as souvenirs.

Textiles and Embroidery: Timeless Elegance

Sorrento's tradition of textile craftsmanship and embroidery is another highlight of the town's artisanal scene, with skilled artisans creating exquisite fabrics and embellishments using traditional techniques. Visitors can explore boutiques and workshops in the historic center and along cobblestone streets, where they can find a variety of handmade textiles, including linens, lace, and embroidered garments. Sorrentine textiles are prized for their quality and elegance, with intricate patterns and delicate embellishments that add a touch of luxury to any home or wardrobe. Visitors can watch artisans at work, observing the meticulous process of weaving, embroidery, and finishing that goes into creating these timeless pieces. Entry to textile workshops is typically free, with the option to purchase handmade textiles as souvenirs or gifts.

Exploring Sorrento's crafts and local artisans offers visitors a unique opportunity to discover the town's cultural heritage and artistic traditions. Whether admiring the intricate wood inlay, browsing handmade ceramics, or sampling artisanal food products, visitors to Sorrento can experience the skill, creativity, and passion that define the town's artisanal scene. So, come explore Sorrento's craft workshops and boutiques – where every piece tells a story of tradition, craftsmanship, and local pride.

7.5. Literary and Historical Figures

Sorrento, with its rich history and cultural heritage, has been home to many notable literary and historical figures whose legacies continue to shape the town's identity. From renowned poets and writers to influential statesmen and artists, Sorrento's literary and historical figures have left an indelible mark on the town and its inhabitants. Exploring the places associated with these figures offers visitors a fascinating journey through Sorrento's past and an opportunity to connect with the stories and personalities that have shaped its history.

Johann Wolfgang von Goethe: A Literary Icon

One of Sorrento's most famous literary visitors was Johann Wolfgang von Goethe, the celebrated German writer and poet who visited the town in the late 18th century. Goethe was inspired by Sorrento's natural beauty and captivating landscapes, which he immortalized in his famous travelogue, "Italian Journey." Visitors can follow in Goethe's footsteps by exploring the places he visited during his time in Sorrento, including the Villa Fiorentino, where he stayed during his visit. The villa is now home to the Museo Correale di Terranova, which houses a collection of art and artifacts that provide insights into Sorrento's cultural heritage. Entry to the Museo Correale di Terranova is €8 for adults and €5 for students, with discounts available for groups and guided tours.

Lucio Anneo Seneca: Philosopher and Statesman

Sorrento's history is also intertwined with that of Lucio Anneo Seneca, the ancient Roman philosopher, and statesman who was born in the nearby town of Pompeii. Seneca spent much of his life in Rome but is believed to have owned a villa in Sorrento, where he may have spent time retreating from the political turmoil of the Roman Empire. Although the exact location of Seneca's villa is unknown, visitors can explore the archaeological ruins of nearby Pompeii and Herculaneum, where traces of ancient Roman life can still be found. Entry to the archaeological sites of Pompeii and

Herculaneum varies depending on the type of ticket purchased and any additional guided tours or exhibitions.

Torquato Tasso: Poet of the Renaissance

Torquato Tasso, the renowned Italian poet of the Renaissance, is another literary figure with connections to Sorrento. Tasso spent time in Sorrento during his tumultuous life, seeking refuge from political persecution and finding inspiration for his epic poem, "Jerusalem Delivered." Visitors can explore the places associated with Tasso in Sorrento, including the Villa Rufolo in nearby Ravello, where Tasso is said to have found inspiration for his poetry. The villa is now a cultural center and tourist attraction, offering panoramic views of the Amalfi Coast and hosting events such as concerts and exhibitions. Entry to the Villa Rufolo is €7 for adults and €5 for students, with discounts available for groups and guided tours.

Norman Douglas: Writer and Traveler

Norman Douglas, the British writer and traveler, is another literary figure who left his mark on Sorrento during the early 20th century. Douglas wrote extensively about his travels in Italy, including his experiences in Sorrento, which he described in his book, "Old Calabria." Visitors can follow in Douglas's footsteps by exploring the streets and landmarks of Sorrento that he mentioned in his writings, such as the historic center and the Villa Comunale. The Villa Comunale is a picturesque park overlooking the Bay of Naples, where visitors can enjoy panoramic views of the coastline and relax amidst lush greenery and colorful flower beds. Entry to the Villa Comunale is free, making it an ideal spot for a leisurely stroll or a peaceful picnic with a view.

Eleanor Clark: Author and Essayist

Eleanor Clark, the American author and essayist, is another literary figure associated with Sorrento. Clark wrote about her experiences living in Sorrento during the mid-20th century in her book, "Rome and a Villa," which recounts her life in Italy and her interactions with local residents. Visitors can explore the places mentioned in Clark's writings, such as the historic center of Sorrento and the nearby town of Positano, which she frequented during her time in the region. In Sorrento, visitors can wander through the narrow streets of the historic center, admiring the colorful buildings and bustling piazzas, and perhaps even stop for a meal at one of the town's traditional trattorias or cafes.

Alfonso Gatto: Poet and Playwright

Alfonso Gatto, the Italian poet and playwright, is one of Sorrento's most beloved literary figures, known for his evocative poetry and lyrical prose. Gatto was born and raised in Sorrento and drew inspiration from the town's landscapes and traditions in his writing. Visitors can explore the places associated with Gatto in Sorrento, including the Piazza Tasso, named after the 16th-century poet Torquato Tasso, and the Villa Fondi, a historic villa overlooking the sea where Gatto is said to have found inspiration for his poetry. The villa now houses a public park and cultural center, offering visitors a peaceful retreat amidst stunning scenery. Entry to the Villa Fondi is free, making it a tranquil spot for a scenic walk.

CHAPTER 8
OUTDOOR ACTIVITIES AND ADVENTURES

8.1. Hiking and Nature Trails

Sorrento, with its stunning coastal cliffs, lush Mediterranean vegetation, and breathtaking views of the Bay of Naples, offers visitors an array of hiking and nature trails to explore its natural beauty. These trails wind through ancient olive groves, fragrant citrus orchards, and picturesque villages, providing opportunities for outdoor adventure and immersion in the region's rich cultural and historical heritage. Several hiking and nature trails are accessible from Sorrento's town center, offering visitors convenient access to the region's natural wonders. One popular trail is the Path of the Gods (Sentiero degli Dei), which starts in the village of Bomerano in the nearby town of Agerola and offers panoramic views of the Amalfi Coast. Another option is the Valle delle Ferriere Nature Reserve, located near the town of Amalfi, where visitors can explore lush forests, cascading waterfalls, and ancient ruins.

Most hiking trails in Sorrento are open year-round, but it's essential to check the specific opening hours and trail conditions before embarking on your adventure. Many trails have no entry fees, allowing visitors to explore the natural beauty of the region without additional costs. However, guided tours and transportation to trailheads may incur fees, so it's advisable to research and plan accordingly.

Why Visit Hiking and Nature Trails in Sorrento

Visiting hiking and nature trails in Sorrento provides a unique opportunity to escape the hustle and bustle of the town center and immerse oneself in the region's pristine landscapes. Whether you're an avid hiker seeking a challenge or a nature lover looking to reconnect with the great outdoors, Sorrento's trails offer something for everyone. From panoramic viewpoints overlooking the Mediterranean Sea to hidden waterfalls and ancient ruins, each trail presents a new adventure waiting to be discovered.

Historical and Cultural Significance

Many of Sorrento's hiking trails pass through areas of historical and cultural significance, providing insights into the region's rich heritage. For example, the Path of the Gods follows an ancient trade route used by shepherds and merchants for centuries, connecting the towns of Agerola and Positano. Along the trail, hikers can encounter historical sites such as ancient watchtowers and medieval chapels, offering glimpses into Sorrento's past. While exploring hiking and nature trails in Sorrento, visitors can engage in a variety of activities to enhance their experience. Hiking enthusiasts can embark on guided tours led by experienced local guides who provide insights into the region's flora, fauna, and geological features. Nature lovers can enjoy birdwatching, photography, and botany excursions, discovering the diverse ecosystems that thrive in Sorrento's coastal and mountainous terrain.

Tips for Visitors

Before setting out on a hiking adventure in Sorrento, it's essential to be prepared and informed. Make sure to wear sturdy hiking shoes, bring plenty of water and snacks, and wear sunscreen and a hat to protect against the sun. Additionally, familiarize yourself with the trail map and terrain, and consider hiring a local guide for added safety and navigation assistance. Finally, respect the environment and follow Leave No Trace principles to preserve Sorrento's natural beauty for future generations to enjoy. Sorrento's hiking and nature trails are accessible by various means of transportation, including public buses, taxis, and private tours. Visitors can reach trailheads by taking a bus from Sorrento's town center to nearby villages such as Agerola, Amalfi, or Positano, where many trails begin. Alternatively, guided tours and transportation services are available for those seeking a hassle-free hiking experience.

Other Essential Information for Visitors

Before embarking on a hiking adventure in Sorrento, it's essential to check the weather forecast and trail conditions, as some trails may be closed or impassable during inclement weather or due to maintenance work. Additionally, be mindful of wildlife and natural hazards such as steep cliffs, slippery terrain, and unstable rocks. Finally, make sure to pack essentials such as a first aid kit, flashlight, and emergency supplies in case of unexpected situation. Exploring hiking and nature trails in Sorrento is a must-see attraction for visitors seeking to experience the region's natural beauty and cultural heritage. With its panoramic views, historical sites, and diverse ecosystems, Sorrento's trails offer endless opportunities for outdoor adventure and exploration. So, lace up your hiking boots, pack your camera, and embark on a journey to discover the hidden gems of Sorrento's great outdoors.

8.2. Water Sports and Beach Activities

Sorrento, with its stunning coastline overlooking the Bay of Naples, offers visitors a wide range of water sports and beach activities to enjoy the Mediterranean Sea to the fullest.

From swimming and sunbathing on pristine beaches to exhilarating water sports such as snorkeling, kayaking, and paddleboarding, Sorrento's coastal waters provide endless opportunities for outdoor adventure and relaxation. Sorrento's beaches and water sports centers are conveniently located along the town's coastline, making them easily accessible from the town center and nearby hotels. Some of the most popular beaches in Sorrento include Marina Grande, Marina Piccola, and Bagni della Regina Giovanna, each offering its unique atmosphere and amenities for beachgoers and water sports enthusiasts.

Most beaches in Sorrento are open to the public throughout the day, with no entry fees required for access. However, certain beach clubs and water sports centers may charge rental fees for equipment such as lounge chairs, umbrellas, and water sports gear. It's essential to check the opening hours and rental prices in advance, especially during peak tourist seasons, to ensure a hassle-free beach experience.

Why Visit Water Sports and Beach Activities in Sorrento

Visiting water sports and beach activities in Sorrento provides visitors with the perfect opportunity to unwind and enjoy the natural beauty of the Mediterranean Sea. Whether you're seeking an adrenaline rush through water sports or simply want to relax on the beach and soak up the sun, Sorrento's coastal offerings cater to all preferences and interests. Additionally, exploring Sorrento's beaches allows visitors to immerse themselves in the region's maritime culture and heritage, as the town has long been a hub for fishing, trade, and maritime exploration.

Historical and Cultural Significance

Sorrento's coastal areas have played a significant role in the region's history and culture, dating back to ancient times. The town's strategic location along the Bay of Naples made it an important port for trade and maritime activities, connecting Sorrento to other cities along the Mediterranean coast. Today, remnants of Sorrento's maritime heritage can be found in its quaint fishing villages, historic harbors, and traditional fishing techniques that continue to be practiced by local fishermen.

Visitors to Sorrento's beaches can enjoy a variety of water sports and beach activities suitable for all ages and skill levels. Some popular activities include swimming and snorkeling in the crystal-clear waters of the Mediterranean Sea, where visitors can discover vibrant marine life and underwater rock formations. For those seeking a more adrenaline-fueled experience, kayaking, paddleboarding, and jet skiing are available, allowing adventurers to explore Sorrento's coastline from a different perspective. Additionally, beachgoers can indulge in leisurely activities such as sunbathing, beach volleyball, or simply strolling along the sandy shores and enjoying panoramic views of the surrounding cliffs and coastline.

Tips for Visitors

Before heading to Sorrento's beaches for water sports and beach activities, it's essential to come prepared and informed. Make sure to pack sunscreen, a hat, sunglasses, and plenty of water to stay hydrated under the Mediterranean sun. Additionally, wear appropriate swimwear and footwear for water sports activities, and consider renting equipment from reputable rental shops along the beach. It's also advisable to check the weather forecast and sea conditions before engaging in water sports to ensure safety and enjoyment during your beach excursion.

Sorrento's beaches and water sports centers are easily accessible from the town center by foot, car, or public transportation. Visitors can take a leisurely stroll along the coastal promenade from the town center to reach popular beaches such as Marina Grande and Marina Piccola. Alternatively, taxis and buses are available for those seeking a more convenient mode of transportation, with designated stops near beach access points. Private tours and boat excursions are also available for visitors looking to explore Sorrento's coastline and nearby islands from the water.

Other Essential Information for Visitors

Before visiting Sorrento's beaches for water sports and beach activities, it's essential to be mindful of local regulations and etiquette to ensure a pleasant experience for everyone. Respect designated swimming areas and safety flags, follow instructions from lifeguards and beach attendants, and dispose of trash responsibly to help preserve Sorrento's pristine coastal environment. Additionally, be mindful of marine life such as jellyfish and sea urchins, and take necessary precautions to avoid encounters or injuries while in the water. Exploring water sports and beach activities in Sorrento is a must-see attraction for visitors seeking to experience the region's natural beauty and maritime culture. With its idyllic beaches, crystal-clear waters, and diverse range of water sports and leisure activities, Sorrento's coastal offerings provide the perfect setting for outdoor adventure and relaxation. So, pack your swimsuit, sunscreen, and sense of adventure, and prepare for an unforgettable beach experience along the stunning shores of Sorrento.

8.3. Boat Tours and Cruises

Sorrento, with its stunning coastal vistas and proximity to iconic landmarks such as Capri, the Amalfi Coast, and the Isle of Ischia, offers visitors the perfect opportunity to explore the Mediterranean Sea through boat tours and cruises. These excursions provide a unique perspective of Sorrento's rugged coastline, hidden coves, and azure waters, making them a must-see attraction for travelers seeking to experience the beauty and charm of the region. Boat tours and cruises in Sorrento depart from the town's main marinas, including Marina Grande and Marina Piccola, as well as from nearby ports such as Marina di Cassano and Marina di Puolo. These marinas are conveniently located within walking distance from the town center, making them easily accessible for visitors staying in Sorrento's hotels and accommodations.

The opening hours of boat tours and cruises in Sorrento vary depending on the season and the type of excursion. Many tour operators offer half-day or full-day cruises, as well as sunset and evening cruises, to accommodate different schedules and preferences. The entry fees for boat tours and cruises vary depending on the duration, itinerary, and inclusions, with prices typically ranging from €50 to €150 per person.

Why Visit Boat Tours and Cruises in Sorrento

Exploring Sorrento's coastline and nearby islands by boat offers visitors an unparalleled opportunity to discover hidden gems and scenic vistas that are inaccessible by land. From cruising along the rugged cliffs of the Amalfi Coast to exploring the sea caves and grottoes of Capri, boat tours and cruises in Sorrento provide unforgettable experiences that showcase the region's natural beauty and cultural heritage.

Historical and Cultural Significance

Sorrento's maritime history dates back thousands of years, with evidence of ancient seafaring activities and trade routes found along its coastline. Boat tours and cruises offer insights into Sorrento's maritime heritage, allowing visitors to explore historic ports, fishing villages, and archaeological sites that have played a significant role in the region's history and culture. Additionally, many boat tours offer guided commentary and historical anecdotes, providing context and perspective on Sorrento's rich maritime traditions.

What to Do on Boat Tours and Cruises

During boat tours and cruises in Sorrento, visitors can engage in a variety of activities and experiences to enhance their journey. Snorkeling and swimming stops allow guests to cool off in the crystal-clear waters of the Mediterranean Sea, while onboard amenities such as sun decks, lounges, and bars provide opportunities for relaxation and socializing. Many boat tours also include visits to iconic landmarks such as the Blue Grotto in Capri, the picturesque town of Positano, and the historic fishing village of Amalfi, allowing guests to explore these destinations from a unique perspective. Before embarking on a boat tour or cruise in Sorrento, it's essential to be prepared and informed to ensure a safe and enjoyable experience. Wear comfortable clothing and footwear suitable for a day at sea, and bring essentials such as sunscreen, sunglasses, a hat, and a camera to capture memorable moments along the way. Additionally, be mindful of seasickness, especially if you're prone to motion sickness, and consider taking precautions such as motion sickness medication or acupressure wristbands.

Finally, respect the marine environment and follow the guidance of the crew to ensure the safety and well-being of all passengers onboard.

Transportation and Getting There

Sorrento's main marinas, including Marina Grande and Marina Piccola, are easily accessible from the town center by foot, taxi, or public transportation. Visitors can also arrange transportation to and from the marinas through their hotel concierge or tour operator. Additionally, private transfers and shuttle services are available for guests staying in nearby towns such as Positano, Amalfi, and Naples, providing convenient access to Sorrento's boat tours and cruises. Before booking a boat tour or cruise in Sorrento, it's essential to research and compare different tour operators, itineraries, and prices to find the best option for your preferences and budget. Consider factors such as the size of the vessel, the duration of the tour, and any additional inclusions or amenities offered onboard. Additionally, check the cancellation policy and refund conditions in case of unforeseen circumstances or changes to your travel plans. Finally, don't forget to check the weather forecast and sea conditions before setting sail to ensure a smooth and enjoyable journey on the Mediterranean Sea.

Exploring boat tours and cruises in Sorrento is a must-see attraction for visitors seeking to experience the region's natural beauty and maritime heritage. Whether cruising along the Amalfi Coast, exploring the sea caves of Capri, or enjoying sunset views of the Bay of Naples, Sorrento's boat tours offer unforgettable experiences that showcase the best of the Mediterranean. So, embark on a maritime adventure and discover the wonders of Sorrento's coastline from the comfort of a boat or yacht.

8.4. Diving and Snorkeling

Diving and snorkeling in Sorrento offer visitors a unique opportunity to explore the vibrant marine life and underwater landscapes of the Mediterranean Sea. With its crystal-clear waters, rich biodiversity, and fascinating underwater rock formations,

Sorrento's coastal areas provide an unforgettable experience for diving and snorkeling enthusiasts of all levels.

Location and Accessibility

Sorrento's diving and snorkeling sites are located along the town's coastline, offering easy access from the town center and nearby marinas. Popular diving and snorkeling spots include the Marine Protected Area of Punta Campanella, the underwater caves of the Regina Giovanna Baths, and the rocky reefs of the Bay of Naples. These sites are accessible by boat or from shore, with many dive centers and snorkeling tour operators offering transportation and equipment rental services. The opening hours of diving and snorkeling sites in Sorrento vary depending on the location and operator. Many dive centers and snorkeling tours operate year-round, with daytime and evening excursions available to accommodate different schedules. The entry fees for diving and snorkeling tours typically include equipment rental, guided instruction, and access to the dive site, with prices ranging from €50 to €100 per person.

Why Visit Diving and Snorkeling in Sorrento

Exploring the underwater world of Sorrento offers visitors a unique opportunity to discover a hidden realm teeming with life and beauty. From colorful coral reefs and schools of tropical fish to ancient shipwrecks and underwater caves, Sorrento's diving and snorkeling sites showcase the region's natural diversity and ecological significance. Whether you're an experienced diver or a novice snorkeler, Sorrento's underwater attractions provide an unforgettable experience that will leave you with lasting memories.

Historical and Cultural Significance

Sorrento's maritime heritage dates back thousands of years, with evidence of ancient seafaring activities and trade routes found along its coastline. Diving and snorkeling in Sorrento allow visitors to explore underwater archaeological sites and artifacts that provide insights into the region's rich history and cultural significance. From Roman ruins and submerged statues to World War II shipwrecks and ancient amphorae, Sorrento's underwater treasures offer a fascinating glimpse into the past.

What to Do in Diving and Snorkeling

During diving and snorkeling excursions in Sorrento, visitors can engage in a variety of activities to enhance their underwater experience. Snorkelers can explore shallow reefs, rocky coves, and coastal lagoons teeming with colorful fish, sea turtles, and other marine life. Divers, on the other hand, can venture deeper into the sea to discover underwater caves, walls, and wrecks inhabited by octopuses, moray eels, and groupers. Many dive centers offer guided tours led by experienced instructors who provide safety briefings, equipment orientation, and insights into the local marine environment.

Tips for Visitors

Before embarking on a diving or snorkeling adventure in Sorrento, it's essential to be prepared and informed to ensure a safe and enjoyable experience. Wear appropriate swimwear and footwear for water activities, and bring essentials such as sunscreen, a hat, sunglasses, and a towel to protect against the sun and dry off afterward. Additionally, listen carefully to the instructions provided by your dive guide or snorkeling instructor, and follow safety protocols to minimize risks and ensure a memorable experience for all participants.

Sorrento's diving and snorkeling sites are easily accessible from the town center by foot, taxi, or public transportation. Many dive centers and snorkeling tour operators offer transportation services from designated meeting points or hotels, making it convenient for visitors to reach the dive sites. Additionally, private charters and boat rentals are available for those seeking a more personalized diving or snorkeling experience, allowing guests to explore Sorrento's underwater world at their own pace.

Other Essential Information for Visitors

Before booking a diving or snorkeling excursion in Sorrento, it's essential to research and compare different tour operators, itineraries, and prices to find the best option for your preferences and budget. Consider factors such as the size of the group, the duration of the tour, and the level of experience required, and communicate any special requests or concerns with the tour operator in advance. Additionally, check the weather forecast and sea conditions before your excursion to ensure optimal diving and snorkeling conditions and prepare accordingly.

Diving and snorkeling in Sorrento offer visitors a thrilling and immersive experience that allows them to discover the wonders of the Mediterranean Sea up close. With its rich biodiversity, historical artifacts, and stunning underwater landscapes, Sorrento's diving and snorkeling sites provide endless opportunities for exploration and discovery. So, don your mask and fins, and dive into the turquoise waters of Sorrento for an unforgettable underwater adventure that will leave you breathless.

8.5. Gardens and Parks

Sorrento, with its mild Mediterranean climate and lush landscapes, is home to several beautiful gardens and parks that offer visitors a tranquil escape from the bustling town center. From historic botanical gardens to scenic coastal parks, these green spaces showcase the region's natural beauty and provide opportunities for relaxation, exploration, and cultural immersion.

Villa Comunale di Sorrento

Villa Comunale di Sorrento, also known as the Sorrento Town Park, is a picturesque public garden located near the town center at Piazza Vittoria. Established in the 19th century, the park features manicured lawns, colorful flowerbeds, and shady groves of trees, offering a peaceful retreat for locals and visitors alike. With its panoramic views of the Bay of Naples and Mount Vesuvius, Villa Comunale di Sorrento is an ideal spot for picnics, leisurely strolls, and enjoying sunset vistas over the sea. The entry fee is absolutely free for everyone.

Villa Fiorentino

Villa Fiorentino is a historic villa and cultural center set amidst lush gardens and citrus groves in the heart of Via Correale, Sorrento. Originally built in the 19th century, the villa now hosts art exhibitions, concerts, and cultural events throughout the year. The gardens surrounding the villa are beautifully landscaped with Mediterranean plants, ornamental fountains, and sculptures, creating a serene oasis in the bustling town center The entry fee ranges as low as €2. Visitors can explore the gardens, admire the artworks on display, and attend cultural performances in this charming setting.

Parco Ibsen

Parco Ibsen is a small public park at Via Ibsen, dedicated to the Norwegian playwright Henrik Ibsen, who spent time in Sorrento during the late 19th century. Located near the Villa Comunale, the park features lush greenery, shaded walkways, and benches where visitors can relax and enjoy views of the surrounding landscape. The park also contains a bust of Ibsen, commemorating his connection to Sorrento and his contribution to literature and the arts. There are no entry fees to be paid.

Museo Correale di Terranova Gardens

The Museo Correale di Terranova Gardens located at Via Correale, 50, Sorrento, is part of a historic villa and museum complex located in the center of Sorrento. The villa's gardens are renowned for their botanical diversity, featuring exotic plants, rare specimens, and fragrant citrus trees. Visitors can stroll through the gardens, admire the colorful blooms, and learn about the flora of the region. The museum also houses a collection of Neapolitan paintings, ceramics, and decorative arts, providing insight into Sorrento's cultural heritage.The Entry fee is €8 (includes museum admission)

Villa Lauro

Villa Lauro is a historic villa and public park located at Via Santa Maria della Pietà, Sorrento. The villa's gardens feature Mediterranean vegetation, shaded pathways, and ornamental ponds, creating a peaceful retreat for visitors to enjoy. The park also offers panoramic views of Sorrento's rooftops and the surrounding countryside, making it a popular spot for photography and relaxation. There are no entry fees.

Giardino della Minerva

Giardino della Minerva is a unique botanical garden located in the historic center of Sorrento at Via San Nicola, 7. Originally created in the 14th century by the local pharmacist, the garden is dedicated to the cultivation of medicinal and aromatic plants used in traditional herbal medicine. With just an entry fee of €5, Visitors can explore the garden's terraced beds, learn about the therapeutic properties of various herbs and spices, and purchase herbal products and souvenirs at the onsite shop. Giardino della Minerva offers a fascinating glimpse into Sorrento's botanical heritage and its connection to the ancient art of herbalism.

Sorrento's gardens and parks offer visitors a delightful blend of natural beauty, cultural heritage, and recreational opportunities. Whether exploring historic villas, strolling through manicured gardens, or admiring panoramic views of the Bay of Naples, these green spaces provide a tranquil escape from the hustle and bustle of the town center. With their diverse botanical collections, scenic landscapes, and cultural significance, Sorrento's gardens and parks are truly a must-see attraction for visitors seeking to experience the charm and beauty of this coastal paradise.

8.6 Family and Kids Friendly Activities

Sorrento, with its charming streets, stunning coastline, and rich cultural heritage, offers a plethora of family and kid-friendly activities that are sure to delight visitors of all ages. From exploring ancient ruins to enjoying thrilling amusement parks,

Sorrento provides endless opportunities for families to create lasting memories together.

Pompeii Archaeological Park

Pompeii, approximately 25 kilometers from Sorrento is an Archaeological park that offers families a fascinating journey back in time to the ancient Roman city that was buried by the eruption of Mount Vesuvius in 79 AD. Kids can explore the well-preserved streets, homes, and public buildings of Pompeii, gaining insight into daily life in ancient times. Guided tours and interactive exhibits are available to enhance the experience and provide context to the archaeological site. The entry fee is €16 (adults), free for children under 18 years old

Sorrento Cooking School

Situated at Via Fuorimura, 12 Sorrento, Cooking School offers families the opportunity to learn the art of Italian cuisine in a fun and interactive environment. Kids can participate in hands-on cooking classes, where they'll learn to prepare traditional dishes such as pizza, pasta, and gelato under the guidance of expert chefs. After the cooking session, families can enjoy a delicious meal together, savoring the fruits of their labor and creating cherished memories. The entry fee varies by class.

Mini Golf Sorrento

Mini Golf Sorrento at Via Nastro Verde Sorrento, offers families a fun-filled day of miniature golf in a picturesque setting overlooking the Bay of Naples. Kids can test their putting skills on the 18-hole course, navigating through water features, obstacles, and themed holes inspired by Sorrento's landmarks. The entry fee is €10 per person (includes equipment rental). The facility also features a snack bar, arcade games, and outdoor seating areas, providing entertainment for the whole family.

Acqua Park Isca

Acqua Park Isca is a water park located in the countryside at Via Cermenna, Casarlano, approximately 15 kilometers from Sorrento, offering families a refreshing escape from the summer heat. Kids can splash and play in the park's pools, water slides, and lazy river, while parents relax on sun loungers or enjoy a picnic in the shaded picnic areas. The entry fee is €15 (adults), €10 (children 4-12 years old). The park also features snack bars, changing facilities, and lifeguards on duty for added safety.

Sorrento Musical

Sorrento Musical is a lively theatrical performance located at Teatro Tasso, Via Fuorimura, showcases the traditional music, dance, and culture of Southern Italy. Families can enjoy an evening of entertainment featuring talented performers, colorful costumes, and captivating storytelling from 9:00 PM - 11:00 PM daily. The show highlights the region's folk traditions, including tarantella dances, Neapolitan songs, and comedic sketches, providing an immersive cultural experience for audiences of all ages. The entry fee ranges from €30 (adults), €15 (children under 12 years old)

Marameo Beach

Located at Via Nastro Verde, Sorrento, opens daily from 9:00 AM - 7:00 PM. The entry fee is free (beach access), rental fees apply for sunbeds and umbrellas. Marameo Beach is a family-friendly beach located within walking distance of Sorrento's town center. Kids can build sandcastles, paddle in the shallow waters, and play beach games while parents relax on sun loungers and soak up the sun.

The beach offers amenities such as showers, changing facilities, and beach bars serving refreshments and snacks, making it a convenient option for families looking to spend a day by the sea.

Sorrento's family and kid-friendly activities offer a perfect blend of entertainment, education, and relaxation for visitors of all ages. Whether exploring ancient ruins, learning to cook Italian cuisine, or enjoying outdoor adventures, families are sure to create unforgettable memories together in this picturesque coastal town. So, pack your bags, gather the family, and embark on an exciting adventure in Sorrento that will leave everyone smiling from ear to ear.

8.7 Activities for Solo Travelers

Sorrento, with its stunning coastal vistas, rich history, and vibrant culture, offers a plethora of activities for solo travelers seeking to immerse themselves in the beauty and charm of this picturesque town. From scenic walks along the coastline to cultural excursions and culinary experiences, Sorrento provides endless opportunities for solo adventurers to explore, relax, and indulge in the local atmosphere.

Walking tours along the scenic coastline

One of the most rewarding activities for solo travelers in Sorrento is taking leisurely walks along the scenic coastline. The coastal paths offer stunning views of the Bay of Naples, Mount Vesuvius, and the rugged cliffs that characterize the Sorrento peninsula. Solo travelers can stroll along the promenades of Marina Grande and Marina Piccola, explore hidden coves and beaches, and admire the colorful fishing boats and luxury yachts that dot the shoreline.

Embarking on a historical walking tour of Sorrento's town center is an excellent way for solo travelers to learn about the town's rich heritage and cultural significance. Guided tours typically include visits to iconic landmarks such as the Cathedral of Saints Philip and James, the Chiostro di San Francesco, and the Vallone dei Mulini. Along the way, travelers can discover hidden gems, narrow cobblestone streets, and charming piazzas while learning about Sorrento's ancient past and its connections to Greek, Roman, and medieval civilizations.

Culinary Delights

Solo travelers can indulge in the culinary delights of Sorrento by participating in wine tasting and culinary experiences offered by local vineyards and restaurants. These experiences typically include guided tastings of regional wines such as Lacryma Christi and Falanghina, accompanied by traditional dishes such as fresh seafood, pasta, and local cheeses. Solo travelers can savor the flavors of Sorrento while enjoying stunning views of the surrounding countryside and vineyards. For solo travelers seeking adventure, a Vespa tour of the Amalfi Coast offers an exhilarating way to explore the scenic roads and picturesque villages of this iconic region. Guided Vespa tours typically depart from Sorrento and follow winding coastal roads to destinations such as Positano, Amalfi, and Ravello. Along the way, travelers can enjoy panoramic views of the Mediterranean Sea, stop for photo opportunities, and explore charming seaside towns at their own pace.

Participating in Cooking classes

Solo travelers can immerse themselves in the culinary traditions of Sorrento by participating in a cooking class and market tour. These hands-on experiences typically begin with a visit to a local market, where travelers can select fresh ingredients and learn about the region's culinary heritage. Back in the kitchen, participants work alongside expert chefs to prepare traditional dishes such as homemade pasta, pizza, and gelato, before sitting down to enjoy their creations with a glass of local wine. Solo travelers can embark on a boat excursion to the nearby island of Capri for a day of exploration and relaxation. Boat tours typically depart from Sorrento port and include stops at iconic landmarks such as the Blue Grotto, the Faraglioni rock formations, and the picturesque town of Anacapri. Travelers can swim in crystal-clear waters, soak up the Mediterranean sun, and explore the island's charming streets and boutiques at their leisure before returning to Sorrento in the evening.

Sorrento offers a wealth of activities for solo travelers seeking adventure, relaxation, and cultural immersion. From coastal walks and historical tours to wine tastings, cooking classes, and boat excursions, there's something for every solo adventurer to enjoy in this enchanting town. With its stunning landscapes, rich history, and warm hospitality, Sorrento provides the perfect destination for solo travelers looking to experience the beauty and charm of the Amalfi Coast.

CHAPTER 9
SHOPPING IN SORRENTO

Click on the Link or Scan the QR Code with a device to view a comprehensive map of Shopping Districts in Sorrento – https://shorturl.at/afiM5

9.1. Boutiques and Fashion Stores

Sorrento, with its picturesque streets and vibrant atmosphere, is not only known for its stunning scenery but also for its thriving fashion scene. From high-end boutiques to charming local stores, Sorrento offers an array of shopping destinations that cater to every style and taste.

Chic Boutique

Chic Boutique, located on the bustling Corso Italia at Corso Italia Sorrento, is a haven for fashion enthusiasts seeking the latest trends and designer labels. The store offers a curated selection of clothing, shoes, and accessories from renowned Italian and international brands. Visitors can browse through racks of stylish dresses, elegant handbags, and statement jewelry, with prices ranging from moderate to high-end. Chic Boutique is open from 10:00 AM to 8:00 PM, making it convenient for shoppers to explore the store at their leisure.

La Dolce Vita

La Dolce Vita is a charming boutique nestled in the historic center of Sorrento at Via San Cesareo, offering a mix of classic elegance and contemporary flair. The store specializes in Italian-made clothing and accessories, including beautifully crafted leather handbags, silk scarves, and linen clothing. Visitors can peruse the collection of timeless pieces, each selected for its quality and craftsmanship. La Dolce Vita is open from 9:00 AM to 7:00 PM, providing ample time for shoppers to indulge in a leisurely shopping experience.

Moda Italia

Moda Italia at Piazza Tasso, Sorrento is a popular destination for fashion-forward shoppers seeking stylish apparel at affordable prices. Situated in the heart of Piazza Tasso, the store offers a diverse range of clothing and accessories for men, women, and children. From casual attire to formal wear, Moda Italia has something for every occasion, with prices catering to budget-conscious shoppers. The store is open from 9:30 AM to 9:00 PM, making it a convenient option for those exploring the town center.

Capri Sandals

Located at Via Luigi de Maio, Sorrento. Capri Sandals specializes in handmade leather sandals crafted by skilled artisans using traditional techniques. Located in a quaint alleyway off Via Luigi de Maio, the store offers a wide selection of sandals in various styles, colors, and sizes. Visitors can customize their sandals with different straps and embellishments, creating a unique and personalized souvenir of their trip to Sorrento. Prices for sandals at Capri Sandals range from affordable to mid-range, with options to suit every budget. The store is open from 10:00 AM to 7:00 PM, allowing shoppers to take their time choosing the perfect pair of sandals.

Sorrento Boutique

Sorrento Boutique is a family-owned shop specializing in locally made products and souvenirs. Situated near the Corso Italia at Via Correale, the store offers a wide range of items, including handmade ceramics, embroidered linens, and hand-painted tiles. Visitors can find unique gifts and mementos to take home as reminders of their time in Sorrento. Prices at Sorrento Boutique vary depending on the item, with options available for every budget. The store is open from 9:00 AM to 8:00 PM, making it convenient for shoppers to drop in during their sightseeing excursions.

Marina Grande Fashion

Marina Grande Fashion is a boutique located near the Marina Grande at Via del Mare Sorrento, offers a selection of resort wear and beach essentials. The store features a range of swimwear, cover-ups, and accessories perfect for a day at the beach or pool. Visitors can browse through racks of colorful kaftans, stylish sunglasses, and trendy beach bags, with prices that cater to all budgets. Marina Grande Fashion is open from 10:00 AM to 6:00 PM, providing shoppers with ample time to shop before heading to the nearby beach.

Getting There and Other Information

Visitors to Sorrento can easily access the boutiques and fashion stores by foot or public transportation. The town center is pedestrian-friendly, with most shops located within walking distance of each other. For those staying outside the town center, taxis and buses are readily available for transportation to and from the shopping areas. When shopping in Sorrento, it's advisable to bring cash as some smaller stores may not accept credit cards. Additionally, bargaining is not common practice in Italy, so be prepared to pay the listed prices for goods and services. Finally, don't forget to check the store's return policy before making a purchase, especially for clothing and accessories. Sorrento's boutiques and fashion stores offer a diverse shopping experience for visitors seeking stylish apparel, accessories, and souvenirs. From upscale boutiques to quaint local shops, there's something for everyone in this charming coastal town. So, whether you're in search of designer labels, handmade sandals, or unique souvenirs, Sorrento's fashion scene has you covered.

9.2. Souvenir Shops and Local Crafts

Sorrento is not only renowned for its breathtaking views and rich history but also for its vibrant culture and local craftsmanship. Visitors to Sorrento have the opportunity to explore a variety of souvenir shops and artisan boutiques, each offering unique treasures and handcrafted goods that serve as lasting mementos of their time in this picturesque town.

Artigianato Sorrentino

Artigianato Sorrentino, located in the heart of Sorrento's historic center on Via San Cesareo, is a treasure trove of local crafts and traditional souvenirs. Visitors can browse through a wide selection of hand-painted ceramics, intricately carved wooden items, and delicate lacework, all crafted by local artisans. Prices at Artigianato Sorrentino vary depending on the item's size and complexity, but there are options available for every budget. The shop is open from 9:00 AM to 8:00 PM, making it convenient for visitors to stop by and explore during their time in Sorrento.

Limoncello di Capri

Limoncello di Capri is a charming boutique located along Corso Italia, Sorrento's main thoroughfare. Specializing in locally made limoncello liqueur and other citrus-infused products, the shop offers a taste of Sorrento's famous lemon groves. Visitors can sample different varieties of limoncello and purchase bottles to take home as souvenirs or gifts. In addition to liqueur, Limoncello di Capri also sells a range of lemon-themed products such as soaps, candles, and chocolates. Prices for limoncello vary depending on the size and brand, with smaller bottles available for around €10 to €20. The boutique is open from 10:00 AM to 9:00 PM, allowing ample time for visitors to indulge in a little lemony delight.

Emporio della Ceramica

Emporio della Ceramica is a boutique specializing in handcrafted ceramics, a traditional art form that has been practiced in Sorrento for centuries. Located on Via Fuorimura, the shop offers a wide range of ceramic items, including plates, bowls, tiles, and decorative ornaments, all adorned with colorful designs inspired by the local landscape and culture. Prices for ceramics at Emporio della Ceramica vary depending on the size and intricacy of the piece, but there are options available to suit every budget. The boutique is open from 9:00 AM to 7:00 PM, providing visitors with ample opportunity to explore and admire the craftsmanship of these beautiful creations.

Cuore di Sorrento

Cuore di Sorrento, situated in the bustling Piazza Tasso, is a charming souvenir shop offering a variety of locally made products and gifts. Visitors can find an array of items, including handmade leather goods, artisanal food products, and decorative items crafted by local artisans. Prices at Cuore di Sorrento vary depending on the item, with options available for every budget. The shop is open from 9:30 AM to 9:00 PM, making it convenient for visitors to explore the offerings at their leisure.

Artesanato Limoncello

Artesanato Limoncello is a boutique specializing in artisanal limoncello liqueur and other citrus-based products. Located on Via Luigi de Maio, the shop offers a wide selection of limoncello varieties, as well as lemon-infused olive oils, jams, and sweets. Visitors can sample different flavors of limoncello and learn about the production process from the knowledgeable staff. Prices for limoncello at Artesanato Limoncello range from €10 to €30, depending on the size and brand. The boutique is open from 10:00 AM to 8:00 PM, providing ample time for visitors to stock up on these zesty delights.

Sorrento Wood Craft

Sorrento Wood Craft is a boutique specializing in handcrafted wooden items, a traditional craft for which Sorrento is famous. Located on Via degli Aranci, the shop offers a range of products including music boxes, jewelry chests, and decorative objects, all intricately carved from fine woods such as walnut, cherry, and olive. Prices for wooden items at Sorrento Wood Craft vary depending on the size and complexity of the piece, with options available for every budget. The boutique is open from 9:00 AM to 7:00 PM, allowing visitors ample time to explore the exquisite craftsmanship on display.

Getting There and Other Information

Visitors to Sorrento can easily access the souvenir shops and local crafts boutiques by foot, as most are located within the town center and are easily reachable from popular landmarks and attractions. Additionally, Sorrento's public transportation system provides convenient access to the town center for those staying in nearby areas. When shopping for souvenirs and local crafts in Sorrento, it's essential to keep in mind that many items are handmade and may vary slightly in size, shape, and color. Visitors should also inquire about shipping options for larger items or purchases made in bulk to ensure safe delivery home. Finally, bargaining is not common practice in Italy, so be prepared to pay the listed prices for goods and services.

Sorrento's souvenir shops and local crafts boutiques offer visitors a delightful array of handcrafted treasures and unique mementos that capture the essence of this charming coastal town. Whether it's hand-painted ceramics, artisanal limoncello, or intricately carved wooden items, there's something for everyone to discover and cherish as a lasting reminder of their time in Sorrento. So, be sure to carve out some time in your itinerary to explore these enchanting shops and bring a piece of Sorrento's craftsmanship home with you.

9.3. Art Galleries and Antique Dealers

Sorrento, with its rich history and stunning landscapes, has long been a haven for artists and collectors alike. From traditional Italian artwork to unique antiques, the town boasts a variety of art galleries and antique dealers where visitors can immerse themselves in the region's cultural heritage and artistic expression.

Galleria D'Arte Sorrento

Galleria D'Arte Sorrento, located on Via San Cesareo, is a premier destination for contemporary art enthusiasts. The gallery showcases a diverse collection of paintings, sculptures, and mixed media artwork created by local and international artists. Visitors can explore a range of styles and techniques, from abstract expressionism to figurative realism, with prices varying depending on the artist and medium. Galleria D'Arte Sorrento is open from 10:00 AM to 8:00 PM, providing ample opportunity for art lovers to browse and discover new favorites.

Antica Sorrento

Antica Sorrento is a renowned antique dealer located along Corso Italia, Sorrento's main shopping street. The shop specializes in antique furniture, decorative objects, and collectibles sourced from Italy and beyond. Visitors can peruse a curated selection of items ranging from vintage chandeliers and ornate mirrors to intricately carved wooden furniture and ancient artifacts. Prices at Antica Sorrento vary depending on the age, rarity, and condition of the items, with options available for both seasoned collectors and casual shoppers. The shop is open from 9:30 AM to 7:30 PM, allowing visitors plenty of time to explore its treasures.

Galeria de Arte La Tana

Galeria de Arte La Tana, situated on Via Fuorimura, is a cozy art gallery specializing in local and regional artwork. The gallery features paintings, prints, and ceramics created by emerging and established artists from Sorrento and the surrounding area. Visitors can admire works inspired by the region's stunning landscapes, vibrant culture, and rich history, with prices ranging from affordable prints to investment-worthy originals. Galeria de Arte La Tana is open from 10:00 AM to 7:00 PM, providing art enthusiasts with the opportunity to explore its diverse collection at their leisure.

Antiquariato Sorrento

Antiquariato Sorrento, located in the historic Piazza Tasso, is a treasure trove of antique finds and vintage collectibles. The shop offers a curated selection of furniture, jewelry, and objets d'art dating from the Renaissance period to the mid-20th century. Visitors can browse through the eclectic mix of items, each with its own unique history and charm. Prices at Antiquariato Sorrento vary depending on the rarity and provenance of the pieces, with options available for every budget. The shop is open from 9:00 AM to 8:00 PM, making it a convenient destination for collectors and casual shoppers alike.

Arte e Antichita Sorrento

Arte e Antichita Sorrento is a boutique art gallery and antique dealer located on Via degli Aranci, a charming street lined with shops and cafes. The gallery showcases a collection of contemporary artwork and antique treasures sourced from Italy and beyond. Visitors can explore paintings, sculptures, and decorative objects, each meticulously curated to reflect the beauty and heritage of Sorrento. Prices at Arte e Antichita Sorrento vary depending on the artist and provenance of the pieces, with options available for every budget. The gallery is open from 9:00 AM to 7:00 PM, providing art enthusiasts with the opportunity to peruse its offerings at their leisure.

La Bottega dell'Arte

La Bottega dell'Arte, situated near the picturesque Marina Grande, is a boutique art gallery specializing in local handicrafts and artisanal goods. The gallery features a diverse collection of ceramics, textiles, and jewelry crafted by skilled artisans from Sorrento and the surrounding region. Visitors can browse through handmade pottery, intricately woven textiles, and one-of-a-kind jewelry pieces, each showcasing the unique craftsmanship of Sorrento's artisans. Prices at La Bottega dell'Arte vary depending on the item and materials used, with options available for every budget. The gallery is open from 10:00 AM to 6:00 PM, providing visitors with the opportunity to explore its offerings before strolling along the nearby waterfront.

Getting There and Other Information

Visitors to Sorrento can easily access the art galleries and antique dealers by foot, as most are located within the town center and are easily reachable from popular landmarks and attractions. Additionally, Sorrento's public transportation system provides convenient access to the town center for those staying in nearby areas. When visiting art galleries and antique dealers in Sorrento, it's essential to inquire about shipping options for larger items or purchases made in bulk to ensure safe delivery home. Visitors should also check the gallery's opening hours and any special exhibitions or events happening during their visit to maximize their experience.

Sorrento's art galleries and antique dealers offer visitors a unique opportunity to immerse themselves in the region's cultural heritage and artistic expression. Whether exploring contemporary artwork or perusing vintage treasures, there's something for every art lover and collector to discover in this charming coastal town. So, be sure to carve out some time in your itinerary to explore these enchanting galleries and bring a piece of Sorrento's artistic legacy home with you.

9.4. Food Markets and Specialty Shops

From fresh produce markets to specialty food shops, the town offers a plethora of options for food enthusiasts to explore and indulge in the flavors of the region.

Mercato Centrale

Mercato Centrale, located in the heart of Sorrento's historic center at Piazza Antonino Persico, is a bustling food market where locals and visitors alike gather to shop for fresh produce, seafood, meats, and more. The market offers a vibrant array of fruits and vegetables, including locally grown lemons, tomatoes, and olives, as well as an assortment of cheeses, cured meats, and freshly caught fish. Prices at Mercato Centrale vary depending on the season and the vendor, with options available to suit every budget. The market is open daily from 7:00 AM to 1:00 PM, providing visitors with the opportunity to explore its offerings and soak up the lively atmosphere.

Emporio La Sorgente

Emporio La Sorgente is a specialty food shop located along Corso Italia, Sorrento's main shopping street. The shop offers a curated selection of gourmet products, including locally made olive oils, balsamic vinegars, pasta, and sauces. Visitors can also find a variety of regional wines, liqueurs, and artisanal sweets, perfect for bringing a taste of Sorrento home with them. Prices at Emporio La Sorgente vary depending on the product and brand, with options available for every budget. The shop is open from 9:00 AM to 8:00 PM, allowing visitors ample time to explore its offerings and sample some of the region's finest culinary delights.

Antica Salumeria Gambardella

Antica Salumeria Gambardella is a historic delicatessen located on Via Fuorimura, just steps away from Sorrento's main square. The shop specializes in gourmet meats, cheeses, and other artisanal products sourced from across Italy. Visitors can browse through an extensive selection of prosciutto, salami, and cheese, as well as homemade preserves, pickles, and condiments. Prices at Antica Salumeria Gambardella vary depending on the product and quality, with options available for every taste and budget. The shop is open from 8:00 AM to 8:00 PM, making it a convenient stop for food enthusiasts looking to stock up on gourmet treats.

Dolceria del Corso

Dolceria del Corso is a charming pastry shop located on Corso Italia, offering a tempting array of sweet treats and desserts. The shop specializes in traditional Italian pastries, including cannoli, sfogliatelle, and pastiera, as well as a variety of cakes, cookies, and gelato. Visitors can indulge their sweet tooth with a selection of freshly baked goods, all made with the finest ingredients and expert craftsmanship. Prices at Dolceria del Corso vary depending on the item and size, with options available for every budget. The shop is open from 9:00 AM to 10:00 PM, allowing visitors to satisfy their cravings for Italian sweets at any time of day.

Fratelli Aurilia

Fratelli Aurilia is a family-owned grocery store located on Via San Cesareo, specializing in local and regional products. The shop offers a diverse range of goods, including olive oils, wines, pasta, sauces, and preserves, all sourced from trusted producers in the area. Visitors can also find a selection of freshly baked bread, pastries, and deli items, perfect for creating a picnic or enjoying a taste of Sorrento at home. Prices at Fratelli Aurilia vary depending on the product and brand, with options available for every budget. The shop is open from 8:00 AM to 9:00 PM, providing visitors with ample time to explore its offerings and stock up on essentials.

La Bottega della Pasta

La Bottega della Pasta is a specialty pasta shop located on Via degli Aranci, offering a variety of fresh and dried pasta made with traditional recipes and techniques. Visitors can choose from a selection of shapes and flavors, including spaghetti, penne, and gnocchi, as well as specialty pastas infused with ingredients such as lemon, squid ink, and saffron. Prices at La Bottega della Pasta vary depending on the type and quantity of

9.5. Shopping Streets and Centers

From charming cobblestone streets lined with boutique shops to modern shopping centers, Sorrento offers a diverse array of shopping experiences for visitors to enjoy. Let's explore six of the most popular shopping streets and centers in Sorrento, each with its unique charm and offerings.

Corso Italia

Corso Italia is Sorrento's main shopping street, bustling with activity and lined with an eclectic mix of shops, cafes, and restaurants. Here, visitors can find everything from high-end fashion boutiques to local artisanal shops selling handmade goods and souvenirs. The street is particularly known for its fashion stores, offering clothing, shoes, and accessories from both Italian and international designers. Prices on Corso Italia vary depending on the shop and the items being sold, with options available for every budget. The street is busiest during the day, but many shops stay open late into the evening, providing ample opportunity for shopping and exploration.

Via San Cesareo

Via San Cesareo is another popular shopping street in Sorrento, known for its charming atmosphere and wide variety of shops and boutiques. Visitors can stroll along the cobblestone street and browse through shops selling everything from handmade ceramics and artisanal crafts to locally produced limoncello and olive oil. The street is also home to several jewelry stores, offering a selection of unique and finely crafted pieces. Prices on Via San Cesareo vary depending on the shop and the items being sold, with options available for every budget. The street is typically busiest during the day, but many shops remain open well into the evening.

Correale di Terranova Museum

The Correale di Terranova Museum, located on Via Correale, is not only a cultural attraction but also a shopping destination. The museum's gift shop offers a selection of locally made souvenirs, including ceramics, postcards, and books about Sorrento's history and culture. Visitors can browse through the shop's offerings and purchase unique mementos to take home with them. Prices in the museum gift shop are reasonable, with options available for every budget. The shop is typically open during the museum's operating hours, allowing visitors to shop before or after exploring the museum's exhibits.

La Ville Shopping Center

La Ville Shopping Center is Sorrento's premier retail destination, offering a modern shopping experience with a variety of stores and amenities. Located on Via degli Aranci, the shopping center is home to both international and Italian brands, including clothing stores, electronics shops, and specialty boutiques. Visitors can shop for fashion, accessories, and gifts, as well as enjoy a meal or a coffee at one of the center's restaurants or cafes. Prices at La Ville Shopping Center vary depending on the store and the items being sold, with options available for every budget. The center is typically open from late morning until late evening, providing visitors with plenty of time to shop and dine.

Viale degli Aranci

Viale degli Aranci is a picturesque street lined with orange trees and charming shops, offering a more relaxed shopping experience away from the hustle and bustle of the town center. Here, visitors can find a variety of shops selling clothing, accessories, and souvenirs, as well as cafes and gelaterias where they can take a break and enjoy a treat. Prices on Viale degli Aranci vary depending on the shop and the items being sold, with options available for every budget. The street is typically quieter than Corso Italia or Via San Cesareo, making it ideal for leisurely shopping and strolling.

Piazza Tasso

Piazza Tasso is the main square in Sorrento and a bustling hub of activity, with shops, cafes, and restaurants surrounding the picturesque square. Visitors can shop for souvenirs, clothing, and gifts at the various shops and boutiques lining the square, or simply sit and enjoy a coffee while taking in the lively atmosphere. Prices in Piazza Tasso vary depending on the shop and the items being sold, with options available for every budget. The square is busiest during the day and into the evening, making it a popular spot for shopping, dining, and people-watching.

Getting There and Other Information

Visitors to Sorrento can easily access the shopping streets and centers by foot, as most are located within the town center and are easily reachable from popular landmarks and attractions. Additionally, Sorrento's public transportation system provides convenient access to the town center for those staying in nearby areas. When shopping in Sorrento, it's essential to keep in mind that many stores may close for a few hours in the afternoon for the traditional Italian siesta. Additionally, visitors should be aware of pickpockets in crowded areas and should keep their belongings secure while shopping.

CHAPTER 10
DAY TRIPS AND EXCURSIONS

10.1. Capri and the Blue Grotto

Nestled in the azure waters of the Tyrrhenian Sea, the island of Capri beckons travelers with its stunning landscapes, rich history, and legendary beauty. One of the most iconic attractions of Capri is the Blue Grotto, a mesmerizing sea cave illuminated by ethereal blue light. A day trip to Capri and the Blue Grotto from Sorrento promises an unforgettable experience, filled with scenic vistas, cultural discoveries, and aquatic adventures.

To embark on this enchanting day trip, visitors can take a ferry from Sorrento to the port of Marina Grande on Capri. The journey typically takes around 20 to 30 minutes, depending on the ferry service and sea conditions. Ferries run regularly throughout the day, providing convenient options for travelers to choose from. Once on Capri, visitors can explore the island's attractions either on foot, by public bus, or by taking a guided tour.

Exploring Capri

Upon arriving in Marina Grande, visitors are greeted by the vibrant harbor lined with colorful fishing boats and bustling waterfront cafes. From there, they can ascend to the charming town of Capri via funicular or by hiking up the picturesque pathways that wind through lemon groves and fragrant gardens. In the town center, visitors can wander through narrow cobblestone streets adorned with bougainvillea, browse chic boutiques, and savor authentic Italian cuisine at local trattorias.

The Blue Grotto Experience

One of the highlights of any visit to Capri is exploring the famed Blue Grotto, a natural sea cave known for its iridescent blue waters. Visitors can access the Blue Grotto by boarding small rowboats, which are guided by experienced local boatmen. Upon entering the cave, visitors are transported into a magical world illuminated by the refracted sunlight, creating a surreal and captivating ambiance. The azure waters, combined with the echoing sound of the waves, create an otherworldly experience that is truly unforgettable. Visitors should be prepared for a short wait to enter the Blue Grotto, as access is subject to weather conditions and sea levels. It is advisable to visit early in the morning to avoid crowds and ensure a smoother experience. Additionally, visitors should wear comfortable clothing and be prepared for the possibility of getting wet during the boat ride to the Blue Grotto. Cameras and smartphones are also recommended to capture the mesmerizing beauty of the cave's interior.

The cost of transportation from Sorrento to Capri varies depending on the ferry service and ticket class chosen. On average, round-trip ferry tickets cost between €30 to €40 per person. Entrance fees to the Blue Grotto and boat tours are additional and typically range from €14 to €18 per person. Visitors should also budget for meals, souvenirs, and any additional activities they wish to partake in while on the island. A day trip to Capri and the Blue Grotto from Sorrento offers an immersive journey into the natural beauty and cultural heritage of this iconic Italian destination. From the charming streets of Capri town to the ethereal wonders of the Blue Grotto, visitors are treated to a sensory feast that will linger in their memories long after they return home. With its breathtaking scenery and enchanting atmosphere, Capri and the Blue Grotto are must-see attractions for anyone exploring the Amalfi Coast region.

10.2. Amalfi Coast and Positano

The Amalfi Coast, with its dramatic cliffs, colorful villages, and panoramic views of the Mediterranean Sea, is undoubtedly one of Italy's most breathtaking destinations. A day trip from Sorrento to the Amalfi Coast and Positano promises travelers an unforgettable adventure filled with stunning landscapes, charming towns, and culinary delights. Embarking on a day trip to the Amalfi Coast and Positano from Sorrento is easily achievable via various transportation options. Visitors can opt to drive along the scenic coastal road, take a bus tour, or hire a private driver. The distance from Sorrento to

Positano is approximately 16 kilometers, with the journey taking around 30 to 45 minutes by car or bus, depending on traffic conditions.

Exploring the Amalfi Coast

As travelers wind their way along the picturesque coastal road, they are treated to breathtaking vistas of sheer cliffs plunging into the azure sea below, dotted with quaint villages clinging to the hillsides. The drive itself is an adventure, with each hairpin turn revealing a new and awe-inspiring panorama. Along the way, visitors can stop at scenic viewpoints to capture the perfect Instagram-worthy snapshot or simply soak in the natural beauty of the coastline.

Discovering Positano

Arriving in Positano, travelers are greeted by the sight of pastel-colored houses cascading down the cliffside, interspersed with vibrant bougainvillea and charming alleyways. Positano's narrow streets are lined with boutiques, cafes, and artisan shops, offering a wealth of opportunities for shopping and exploration. Visitors can stroll along the bustling promenade, relax on the picturesque beaches, or climb the steep steps to the Church of Santa Maria Assunta for panoramic views of the town and sea. The best time to visit the Amalfi Coast and Positano is during the spring and fall months when the weather is mild, and the crowds are fewer. Summer, while beautiful, can be quite busy and hot, with peak tourist season lasting from June to August. Travelers should be prepared for narrow roads and limited parking in Positano, as well as steep staircases and inclines throughout the town. Comfortable walking shoes and plenty of water are essential for exploring the hilly terrain and navigating the cobblestone streets.

The cost of transportation from Sorrento to the Amalfi Coast and Positano varies depending on the chosen method of travel. Ferry tickets typically range from €15 to €20 per person each way, while bus tours and private drivers may cost between €30 to €50 per person for a full-day excursion. Visitors should also budget for any additional expenses, such as meals, souvenirs, and entrance fees to attractions. For travelers seeking a more leisurely experience, boat tours are available from Sorrento to Positano, allowing passengers to enjoy the stunning coastal scenery from the water. It is advisable to book transportation and tours in advance, especially during the peak tourist season, to ensure availability and secure the best prices. Visitors should also check the weather forecast before embarking on their day trip, as inclement weather can affect visibility and sea conditions along the coast.

A day trip to the Amalfi Coast and Positano from Sorrento is a quintessential Italian experience, offering travelers a taste of la dolce vita amidst some of the most breathtaking scenery in the world. Whether winding along the coastal road or exploring the charming streets of Positano, visitors are sure to be captivated by the beauty and romance of this iconic destination. So, pack your camera, lace up your walking shoes, and prepare to embark on a memorable journey along the stunning Amalfi Coast.

10.3. Pompeii and Herculaneum

Pompeii and Herculaneum stand as haunting reminders of the power of nature and the resilience of humanity. These ancient cities, frozen in time by the catastrophic eruption of Vesuvius in 79 AD, offer visitors a rare glimpse into the daily lives of the ancient Romans. A day trip from Sorrento to Pompeii and Herculaneum is a journey into history, culture, and the awe-inspiring forces of nature. Pompeii and Herculaneum are easily accessible from Sorrento by various means of transportation. Visitors can take a regional train from Sorrento to Naples, then transfer to the Circumvesuviana train line, which stops directly at both Pompeii and Herculaneum. The distance from Sorrento to Pompeii is approximately 26 kilometers, with the journey by train taking around 30 to 40 minutes. The distance from Sorrento to Herculaneum is slightly shorter, at around 22 kilometers, with a similar travel time.

Exploring Pompeii

Upon arrival in Pompeii, visitors are transported back in time to the bustling streets and grandiose villas of this ancient Roman city. The archaeological site of Pompeii is vast, covering an area of over 150 acres, and is home to an array of well-preserved ruins, including temples, baths, theaters, and residential buildings. Visitors can wander through the ancient streets, marvel at the intricate frescoes and mosaics that adorn the walls of the villas, and imagine life in Pompeii before the eruption.

Discovering Herculaneum

A short train ride from Pompeii lies the archaeological site of Herculaneum, a smaller but equally captivating ancient city. Unlike Pompeii, which was buried under layers of volcanic ash and pumice, Herculaneum was engulfed by a pyroclastic flow, preserving many of its buildings and artifacts in astonishing detail. Visitors to Herculaneum can explore well-preserved homes, shops, and public buildings, gaining insight into the daily lives of its inhabitants before the eruption. The best time to visit Pompeii and Herculaneum is during the spring or fall months when the weather is mild, and the sites are less crowded. Summer can be hot and crowded, especially in the middle of the day, so it's advisable to visit early in the morning or late in the afternoon to avoid the heat and crowds. Comfortable walking shoes, a hat, sunscreen, and plenty of water are essential for exploring the expansive archaeological sites.

The cost of transportation from Sorrento to Pompeii and Herculaneum is relatively affordable. Train tickets on the Circumvesuviana line typically cost around €3 to €5 per person each way, depending on the class of service and the destination. Entrance fees to the archaeological sites are additional and vary depending on the type of ticket purchased. Combination tickets, which include admission to both Pompeii and Herculaneum, are available for a discounted price.

Additional Information

Visitors should allocate several hours to explore each site thoroughly, as both Pompeii and Herculaneum are vast archaeological complexes with numerous points of interest. Guided tours are available at both sites and are highly recommended for those seeking a deeper understanding of the history and significance of these ancient cities. Audio guides are also available for rent and provide informative commentary in multiple languages.

A day trip to Pompeii and Herculaneum from Sorrento is a journey into the heart of ancient history, offering visitors a fascinating glimpse into the lives of the Romans before the catastrophic eruption of Mount Vesuvius. From the grandeur of Pompeii's ruins to the intimate charm of Herculaneum's streets, these archaeological sites are testament to the enduring legacy of a civilization lost to time. So, lace up your sandals, pack your camera, and prepare to embark on a journey through the ancient past of Pompeii and Herculaneum.

10.4. Naples and Its Attractions

Naples, the vibrant capital of Italy's Campania region, is a city steeped in history, culture, and culinary delights. A day trip from Sorrento to Naples offers visitors the opportunity to explore iconic landmarks, indulge in authentic Neapolitan cuisine, and immerse themselves in the bustling atmosphere of this dynamic city. Naples is conveniently located just a short distance from Sorrento, making it easily accessible for a day trip. Visitors can take a regional train from Sorrento to Naples, with the journey typically lasting around 1 to 1.5 hours, depending on the type of train and the schedule. Alternatively, buses and organized tours also offer transportation options for travelers looking to explore Naples and its attractions.

Exploring Naples

Upon arrival in Naples, visitors are greeted by the city's lively streets, colorful buildings, and rich cultural heritage. Naples is home to a wealth of attractions, including historic landmarks, museums, and vibrant neighborhoods. One of the city's most iconic sites is the historic center, a UNESCO World Heritage Site known for its narrow streets, ancient churches, and bustling piazzas. Visitors can wander through the Spaccanapoli district, explore the underground tunnels of Napoli Sotterranea, or marvel at the opulent architecture of the Royal Palace of Naples.

Culinary Delights

No visit to Naples would be complete without sampling the city's famous culinary delights. Naples is the birthplace of pizza, and visitors can indulge in authentic Neapolitan pizza at one of the city's many pizzerias. From traditional margherita to creative gourmet toppings, Naples offers a pizza experience like no other. Visitors can also satisfy their sweet tooth with sfogliatelle, pastiera, and other traditional pastries at local bakeries and cafes.

Museums and Cultural Attractions

Naples boasts a rich cultural heritage, with numerous museums and galleries showcasing its artistic and historical treasures. Art enthusiasts can visit the National Archaeological Museum, home to an extensive collection of Roman and Greek artifacts, including treasures from Pompeii and Herculaneum. History buffs can explore the Castel Nuovo, a medieval fortress overlooking the Bay of Naples, or visit the Certosa di San Martino, a former monastery with panoramic views of the city.

Best Time to Visit

The best time to visit Naples is during the spring or fall months, when the weather is mild, and the city is less crowded. Summer can be hot and humid, with temperatures often reaching into the 30s Celsius (90s Fahrenheit), making it less comfortable for sightseeing. Winter can be rainy, but the city's attractions are less crowded, and visitors can still enjoy the city's cultural offerings. The cost of transportation from Sorrento to Naples varies depending on the mode of transportation chosen. Train tickets typically cost between €5 to €10 per person each way, depending on the type of train and the class of service. Bus tickets and organized tours may also be available for a similar price, depending on the provider and the itinerary.

Visitors should be aware that Naples is a bustling city with heavy traffic and limited parking, so driving may not be the most convenient option for exploring the city. Instead, travelers can take advantage of Naples' efficient public transportation system, which includes buses, trams, and the metro. It's also a good idea to wear comfortable walking shoes, as many of Naples' attractions are best explored on foot. A day trip to Naples from Sorrento offers visitors a tantalizing glimpse into the vibrant culture, rich history, and culinary delights of one of Italy's most dynamic cities. From exploring ancient ruins to savoring authentic Neapolitan cuisine, Naples has something to offer every traveler. So, pack your appetite, lace up your walking shoes, and prepare to embark on a memorable journey through the heart of Naples.

10.5. Ischia and Thermal Spas

Ischia, the largest island in the Bay of Naples, is renowned for its natural thermal spas, lush landscapes, and picturesque coastal towns. A day trip from Sorrento to Ischia offers visitors the chance to unwind in the island's rejuvenating thermal waters, explore charming villages, and soak up the Mediterranean sun. Ischia is located approximately 35 kilometers west of Sorrento and is accessible by ferry or hydrofoil. Visitors can take a ferry from Sorrento to Ischia Porto, the island's main port, with the journey typically lasting around 1 to 1.5 hours, depending on the type of vessel and sea conditions. Ferries run regularly throughout the day, providing convenient options for travelers.

Exploring Ischia

Upon arrival in Ischia Porto, visitors are greeted by the bustling harbor, lined with colorful fishing boats and waterfront cafes. From there, travelers can explore the island's attractions, including its renowned thermal spas, scenic beaches, and historic landmarks. Ischia is home to numerous thermal parks and spas, where visitors can relax in natural hot springs, indulge in spa treatments, and enjoy panoramic views of the Mediterranean Sea.

Relaxing in Thermal Spas

Ischia's thermal spas are among the island's most popular attractions, drawing visitors from around the world seeking relaxation and rejuvenation. The island's thermal waters are rich in minerals and are believed to have healing properties for various ailments. Visitors can soak in thermal pools, indulge in mud baths, and enjoy a range of wellness treatments, from massages to hydrotherapy sessions.

Exploring Coastal Villages

In addition to its thermal spas, Ischia is home to a number of charming coastal villages, each with its own unique character and attractions. Visitors can wander through the narrow streets of Ischia Ponte, home to the historic Castello Aragonese, a medieval castle perched on a rocky islet. In Forio, travelers can admire the elegant architecture of the Church of Soccorso and stroll along the picturesque seafront promenade.

The best time to visit Ischia and its thermal spas is during the shoulder seasons of spring and fall, when the weather is mild, and the island is less crowded. Summer can be hot and crowded, especially in July and August, when tourists flock to the island for its beaches and thermal waters. Winter is also a good time to visit, as the island's thermal spas offer a warm escape from the colder weather.

Cost of Transportation

The cost of transportation from Sorrento to Ischia varies depending on the type of vessel and class of service chosen. Ferry tickets typically range from €20 to €30 per person each way, depending on the ferry company and the type of ticket purchased. Hydrofoil tickets may be slightly more expensive but offer faster travel times. Visitors should also budget for any additional expenses, such as meals, spa treatments, and entrance fees to thermal parks. Visitors should be aware that some thermal spas may have specific dress codes or require reservations for spa treatments, especially during peak tourist season. It's also a good idea to bring swimwear, a towel, and sunscreen for a day of relaxation in the thermal pools. Additionally, travelers should check the ferry schedules in advance and arrive at the port early to ensure a smooth journey to Ischia.

A day trip to Ischia and its thermal spas from Sorrento offers visitors a blissful escape to an island paradise, where relaxation, rejuvenation, and natural beauty await. From soaking in thermal waters to exploring charming coastal villages, Ischia is the perfect destination for travelers seeking tranquility and wellness amidst the stunning landscapes of the Bay of Naples. So, pack your swimsuit, prepare to unwind, and embark on a memorable journey to the enchanting island of Ischia.

CHAPTER 11
ENTERTAINMENT AND NIGHTLIFE

11.1. Bars and Cocktail Lounges

Click on the Link or Scan the QR Code with a device to view a comprehensive map of Bars and Cocktail Lounges in Sorrento – https://shorturl.at/birU7

As a seasoned traveler and author, I understand the importance of experiencing a destination's nightlife firsthand. Sorrento, with its charming streets and lively atmosphere, offers a plethora of bars and cocktail lounges where travelers can unwind, socialize, and savor the local flavors. Let me take you on a journey through Sorrento's vibrant nightlife scene, where each establishment tells its own story and leaves a lasting impression on its patrons.

Sip and Savor at La Stanza Del Gusto

Nestled in the heart of Sorrento's historic center, La Stanza Del Gusto is a cozy and inviting bar known for its impeccable cocktails and warm ambiance. As you step inside, you're greeted by the aroma of freshly squeezed citrus and the sound of laughter and conversation. The bartenders here are true artisans, crafting each drink with precision and care. From classic Negronis to inventive creations featuring local limoncello, every sip is a delight for the senses. Prices are reasonable, and the intimate setting makes it the perfect spot for a romantic evening or a relaxed catch-up with friends.

Dance the Night Away at Fauno Notte Club

For those seeking a more lively atmosphere, Fauno Notte Club is the place to be. Located just a short walk from Piazza Tasso, this energetic nightclub pulses with music and energy late into the night. Step onto the dance floor and let the rhythm move you as DJs spin the latest hits and classic favorites. The club's vibrant lighting and stylish decor create an electrifying ambiance, drawing in locals and visitors alike. Entry fees are modest, and the drinks flow freely, ensuring a memorable night out on the town.

Unwind with Panoramic Views at Roof Garden Sorrento

Perched atop a historic building overlooking the Bay of Naples, Roof Garden Sorrento offers a one-of-a-kind setting for cocktails with a view. Ascend the stairs to the rooftop terrace and prepare to be dazzled by the breathtaking panorama stretching out before you. Whether you're enjoying a sunset aperitivo or gazing out at the twinkling lights of the city below, the experience is nothing short of magical. Prices are slightly higher here, but the unparalleled views make it well worth it for a special occasion or a memorable night out.

Discover Hidden Gems at Bar Syrenuse

Tucked away down a narrow alleyway, Bar Syrenuse exudes an air of mystery and intrigue. Step inside and you'll find yourself transported to another time, with its dim lighting, plush furnishings, and eclectic decor. This intimate bar is a favorite among locals, who come here to unwind after a long day and enjoy the carefully curated selection of cocktails and spirits. Prices are reasonable, and the atmosphere is relaxed and convivial, making it the perfect spot to escape the hustle and bustle of the main thoroughfares.

Indulge in Luxury at Franco's Bar

For a taste of luxury, look no further than Franco's Bar, located within the prestigious Grand Hotel Excelsior Vittoria. Situated on a cliff overlooking the Mediterranean Sea, this elegant establishment exudes old-world charm and sophistication. Sink into a plush armchair on the terrace and sip on a signature cocktail crafted by the expert bartenders.

While prices are on the higher end, the impeccable service and stunning views more than justify the expense, making it a must-visit destination for discerning travelers.

Soak Up the Bohemian Vibes at Bar Sedile Dominova

Located in the historic Sedile Dominova building, Bar Sedile Dominova is a hidden gem beloved by locals and travelers alike. Step inside and you'll find yourself surrounded by exposed stone walls, flickering candlelight, and eclectic artwork adorning the walls. The atmosphere here is laid-back and bohemian, with live music adding to the ambiance on select nights. Prices are reasonable, and the extensive drink menu features everything from artisanal cocktails to local wines and craft beers. Whether you're looking for a quiet evening of conversation or a lively night out, Bar Sedile Dominova offers something for everyone.

Sorrento's bars and cocktail lounges offer a diverse array of experiences, from intimate hideaways to pulsating nightclubs. As a veteran traveler and author, I can attest to the allure of Sorrento's vibrant nightlife scene, where each establishment tells its own story and leaves a lasting impression on its patrons. So, whether you're sipping cocktails with a view or dancing the night away, Sorrento's bars and cocktail lounges are sure to leave you with memories to last a lifetime.

11.2. Live Music and Performances

As an avid traveler and author with a passion for firsthand experiences, I invite you to discover the vibrant nightlife of Sorrento, where live music and performances breathe life into the city's enchanting atmosphere. Let me take you on a journey through six remarkable locations where you can indulge in the soulful melodies and captivating rhythms that define Sorrento's entertainment scene.

Piazza Tasso

Located in the heart of Sorrento's historic center, Piazza Tasso is a bustling square that serves as the epicenter of the city's nightlife. Here, under the twinkling lights and starry skies, you'll find an array of outdoor cafes and bars offering live music performances throughout the evening. From traditional Italian folk songs to contemporary covers, the music in Piazza Tasso captures the essence of Sorrento's vibrant culture.

Tasso Theatre

Nestled amidst the charming cobblestone streets of Sorrento, Tasso Theatre is a cultural hub that showcases a diverse range of live performances, including music, theater, and dance. With its intimate setting and historic charm, Tasso Theatre offers visitors a unique opportunity to immerse themselves in the rich artistic heritage of Sorrento. Tickets prices vary depending on the performance, but the experience is worth every penny.

Fauno Bar

For a more laid-back atmosphere and intimate live music experience, head to Fauno Bar, a cozy venue tucked away in the heart of Sorrento's old town. Here, you can unwind with a glass of local wine or a refreshing cocktail while enjoying live music performances by talented local musicians. The relaxed ambiance and friendly staff make Fauno Bar a favorite among locals and visitors alike.

Villa Fiorentino

Situated amidst lush ardens overlooking the Bay of Naples, Villa Fiorentino is a breathtaking setting for outdoor concerts and performances. Throughout the summer months, the villa hosts a series of open-air concerts featuring classical music, opera, and jazz. With its stunning views and serene ambiance, Villa Fiorentino offers a truly magical experience for music lovers of all ages.

Foreigners Club

Perched on the cliffs overlooking the azure waters of the Mediterranean Sea, the Foreigners Club is a sophisticated venue known for its elegant ambiance and live music events. Here, you can enjoy performances by local bands and artists while savoring gourmet cuisine and fine wines. The club's panoramic terrace offers sweeping views of the coastline, making it the perfect spot for a romantic evening out.

Terrazza Bosquet

For a truly unforgettable dining experience accompanied by live music, head to Terrazza Bosquet, a rooftop restaurant located in the heart of Sorrento. As you savor delectable Italian cuisine prepared with locally sourced ingredients, you'll be serenaded by live musicians playing traditional Neapolitan tunes. With its stunning views of the Gulf of Naples and Mount Vesuvius, Terrazza Bosquet is sure to leave a lasting impression.

Sorrento's live music and performance venues offer a captivating blend of tradition, culture, and entertainment that is sure to enchant visitors from around the world. Whether you're sipping cocktails in Piazza Tasso, attending a concert at Villa Fiorentino, or enjoying a romantic dinner at Terrazza Bosquet, Sorrento's nightlife scene promises an unforgettable experience that will leave you longing to return again and again. So, come immerse yourself in the soulful sounds of Sorrento and let the music transport you to a world of beauty and enchantment.

11.3. Nightclubs and Dance Venues

As a seasoned traveler and author who values firsthand experiences, let me introduce you to the vibrant nightlife of Sorrento, where pulsating beats and electrifying energy await at every turn. From chic nightclubs overlooking the Mediterranean to lively dance venues in the heart of the city, Sorrento's nightlife scene offers an unforgettable journey into the realm of music and dance.

Africana Famous Club

Located along the stunning Amalfi Coast, Africana Famous Club is a legendary nightclub that has been a favorite destination for partygoers since the 1960s. Nestled in a natural cave carved into the cliffs, this iconic venue offers breathtaking views of the sea and stars as you dance the night away to the beats of top DJs and live bands. Prices for entry vary depending on the night and special events, but the experience of dancing in a cave overlooking the Mediterranean is truly priceless.

Florida Club

For those seeking a more intimate and upscale nightlife experience, look no further than the Florida Club. Situated in the heart of Sorrento's historic center, this chic nightclub boasts stylish decor, state-of-the-art sound systems, and an impressive lineup of DJs spinning the latest hits. With its glamorous ambiance and VIP bottle service, the Florida Club is the perfect destination for a night of dancing and revelry. Entry prices typically range from €20 to €30, with VIP packages available for those looking to splurge on a special night out.

Bar Olympus

Tucked away in a historic building just steps from Piazza Tasso, Bar Olympus offers a unique blend of live music, DJ sets, and themed parties that cater to a diverse crowd of locals and tourists alike. With its eclectic decor and laid-back atmosphere, this beloved venue is the perfect spot to unwind with a cocktail or get your groove on to the sounds of house, techno, and hip-hop. Entry is usually free, making Bar Olympus a budget-friendly option for a night of fun and dancing in Sorrento.

Seven Club

Situated on the outskirts of Sorrento, Seven Club is a sprawling nightlife complex that features multiple dance floors, outdoor terraces, and VIP lounges overlooking the Bay of Naples. With its sleek design and cutting-edge lighting effects, Seven Club offers an immersive clubbing experience unlike any other in the area. Entry prices vary depending on the night and special events, but the opportunity to dance under the stars with panoramic views of the coastline is well worth it.

Club Deja Vu

Experience the magic of Sorrento's nightlife at Club Deja Vu, a trendy venue known for its lively atmosphere and energetic dance floor. Located in the heart of the city, this vibrant club attracts a diverse crowd of locals and visitors who come together to dance until the early hours of the morning. With its rotating lineup of DJs and themed parties, Club Deja Vu offers an exciting nightlife experience that keeps guests coming back for more. Entry prices typically range from €15 to €25, with drink specials and discounts available for early birds.

La Piazzetta Disco Pub

For a taste of Sorrento's laid-back nightlife scene, head to La Piazzetta Disco Pub, a cozy venue located in the historic center of the city. With its retro decor and retro music, this charming pub offers a nostalgic trip back in time to the golden era of disco. Sip on cocktails and mingle with locals as you dance to the sounds of classic hits and timeless tunes. Entry is usually free, making La Piazzetta Disco Pub a relaxed and budget-friendly option for a night out in Sorrento.

Sorrento's nightclubs and dance venues offer a dynamic and exhilarating nightlife experience that is sure to leave you enchanted. Whether you're dancing in a cliffside cave overlooking the sea or grooving to the beats of a retro disco, Sorrento's nightlife scene promises an unforgettable journey into the heart of Italian culture and entertainment. So, come join the party and let the rhythms of the night sweep you away on a dance-filled adventure in Sorrento.

11.4. Cultural Events and Festivals

As a seasoned traveler and passionate author who values firsthand experiences, I'm excited to introduce you to the vibrant cultural scene of Sorrento. Nestled along the stunning Amalfi Coast, Sorrento is not only known for its breathtaking landscapes but also for its rich cultural heritage and lively festivals. Join me as we explore six enchanting locations where you can immerse yourself in the unique cultural events and festivals that make Sorrento come alive.

Tasso Square: A Hub of Cultural Activity

Located in the heart of Sorrento's historic center, Piazza Tasso serves as a vibrant hub for cultural events and festivals throughout the year. From traditional folk celebrations to contemporary art exhibitions, there's always something exciting happening in this bustling square. Visitors can stroll through open-air markets, enjoy street performances by local artists, or simply soak up the lively atmosphere while sipping espresso at one of the many cafes.

Villa Comunale: A Garden of Delights

Situated overlooking the Bay of Naples, Villa Comunale is a picturesque park that hosts a variety of cultural events and festivals. With its manicured gardens, sweeping sea views, and majestic palm trees, it provides a stunning backdrop for outdoor concerts, theater performances, and art installations. Visitors can attend music festivals, film screenings, and food fairs while enjoying the tranquil beauty of this enchanting oasis.

Sorrento Cathedral: A Historic Setting for Cultural Events

Sorrento Cathedral, with its striking façade and ornate interior, is not only a place of worship but also a venue for cultural events and festivals. Throughout the year, the cathedral hosts concerts, choir performances, and religious processions that celebrate Sorrento's rich religious heritage. Visitors can admire the stunning architecture of the cathedral while experiencing the soul-stirring music and traditions of the local community.

Chiostro di San Francesco: A Hidden Gem

Tucked away in the heart of Sorrento's old town, Chiostro di San Francesco is a hidden gem that hosts a variety of cultural events and exhibitions. This historic cloister, with its elegant columns and peaceful courtyard, provides an intimate setting for art shows, photography exhibitions, and literary readings. Visitors can escape the hustle and bustle of the city and immerse themselves in the tranquility and creativity of this enchanting space.

Museo Correale di Terranova: A Cultural Oasis

For art enthusiasts, Museo Correale di Terranova offers a unique cultural experience in Sorrento. This museum, housed in a beautiful villa overlooking the Gulf of Naples, showcases an impressive collection of paintings, sculptures, and decorative arts from the 17th to the 19th centuries. In addition to its permanent collection, the museum hosts temporary exhibitions, lectures, and workshops that provide insight into Sorrento's artistic heritage.

Ravello Festival: A Celebration of Music and Arts

While technically located in the nearby town of Ravello, the Ravello Festival is a must-visit cultural event for visitors staying in Sorrento. Held annually from June to September, this world-renowned festival features a diverse program of classical music concerts, dance performances, and theatrical productions. Set against the backdrop of Ravello's stunning villas and gardens, the festival offers a truly unforgettable cultural experience that celebrates the beauty and creativity of the Amalfi Coast.

Sorrento's cultural events and festivals offer visitors a unique opportunity to immerse themselves in the rich heritage and vibrant arts scene of this charming coastal town. Whether you're wandering through Piazza Tasso, admiring the artwork at Museo

Correale di Terranova, or attending a concert at Villa Comunale, Sorrento's cultural offerings promise to inspire, enlighten, and entertain. So, come discover the magic of Sorrento's cultural events and festivals, and let your senses be captivated by the beauty and creativity that abound in this enchanting destination.

11.5. Evening Tours and Experiences

From twilight strolls through historic streets to captivating cultural performances under the stars, Sorrento's nightlife offers a tapestry of unforgettable moments waiting to be woven into your travel memories.

Sorrento Twilight Walking Tour

Step into the enchanting world of Sorrento's evening ambiance with a twilight walking tour through its historic streets. Led by knowledgeable local guides, these tours take you on a journey through Sorrento's storied past, illuminated by the soft glow of street lamps and the twinkling lights of bustling cafes. As you wander through ancient alleyways and charming piazzas, you'll uncover hidden gems and architectural marvels that reveal the city's rich cultural heritage. Prices for these tours typically range from €20 to €30 per person, offering exceptional value for an immersive cultural experience.

Wine Tasting at Sunset

Indulge your senses with a magical evening of wine tasting against the backdrop of Sorrento's breathtaking sunset views. Several wineries in the Sorrento region offer evening tours and tastings where you can sample a variety of local wines paired with artisanal cheeses and savory snacks. From crisp whites to robust reds, each sip transports you deeper into the essence of Sorrento's terroir. Prices for wine tasting experiences vary depending on the winery and the selection of wines offered, but the opportunity to savor the flavors of the region is priceless.

Sunset Boat Cruise along the Amalfi Coast

Experience the golden hour like never before with a sunset boat cruise along the stunning Amalfi Coast. Departing from Sorrento's marina, these evening excursions take you on a scenic journey past rugged cliffs, hidden coves, and picturesque villages bathed in the warm glow of the setting sun. As you sip champagne and nibble on local delicacies, you'll witness nature's masterpiece unfold before your eyes. Prices for sunset boat cruises vary depending on the duration and type of vessel, but the memories you'll create are worth every euro.

Nighttime Vespa Tour of Sorrento

Channel your inner Italian with a thrilling nighttime Vespa tour of Sorrento's winding roads and panoramic viewpoints. Led by expert guides, these tours offer a unique perspective of the city's landmarks and coastal scenery illuminated against the night sky. Feel the cool breeze on your face as you zip through the streets, stopping at scenic overlooks and hidden gems along the way. Prices for Vespa tours typically range from €50 to €80 per person, including rental of the scooter and safety equipment.

Traditional Neapolitan Music Concert

Immerse yourself in the soul-stirring melodies of traditional Neapolitan music with an evening concert at one of Sorrento's historic venues. From hauntingly beautiful ballads to lively tarantellas, these performances showcase the rich musical heritage of the region. Whether held in a grand theater or an intimate courtyard, each concert transports you to a bygone era filled with passion and emotion. Ticket prices vary depending on the venue and the artist performing, but the experience of witnessing a live Neapolitan music performance is priceless.

Nighttime Food Tour of Sorrento

Savor the flavors of Sorrento after dark with a nighttime food tour that takes you on a culinary journey through the city's gastronomic delights. Led by expert food guides, these tours introduce you to local delicacies and hidden gems, from street food stalls to family-run trattorias. Sample freshly caught seafood, authentic Neapolitan pizza, and delectable desserts as you explore Sorrento's vibrant food scene under the stars. Prices for food tours vary depending on the number of tastings included and the duration of the tour, but the opportunity to indulge in Sorrento's culinary treasures is worth every euro. Sorrento's evening tours and experiences offer a captivating blend of culture, cuisine, and natural beauty that promises to enchant travelers of all ages. Whether you're sipping wine at sunset, cruising along the Amalfi Coast, or savoring the flavors of traditional Neapolitan cuisine, each experience invites you to immerse yourself in the magic of Sorrento's nightlife and create memories that will last a lifetime. So, come join the adventure and let Sorrento's evening charm cast its spell on you.

CONCLUSION AND INSIDER TIPS FOR VISITORS

As we come to the end of this journey through Sorrento, I hope you've been captivated by the beauty, history, and culture that this enchanting destination has to offer. As a veteran traveler and author who believes in the power of firsthand experiences, I understand the importance of insider tips to ensure that your visit to Sorrento is nothing short of extraordinary. So, before you embark on your adventure, let me share some final insights and recommendations to help you make the most of your time in this remarkable corner of Italy.

Embrace the Pace of Italian Life

One of the most magical aspects of Sorrento is its relaxed and unhurried pace of life. Take the time to slow down, savor the moment, and immerse yourself in the rhythm of Italian culture. Whether you're enjoying a leisurely meal at a local trattoria or strolling along the sun-drenched streets, allow yourself to embrace the laid-back charm of Sorrento.

Explore Beyond the Tourist Hotspots

While Sorrento's iconic landmarks and attractions are certainly worth visiting, don't be afraid to venture off the beaten path and explore the lesser-known corners of the city. Wander through the narrow alleys of the historic center, discover hidden gems tucked away in secluded piazzas, and strike up conversations with locals to uncover hidden treasures that aren't found in guidebooks.

Sample the Flavors of Sorrento

No visit to Sorrento is complete without indulging in its culinary delights. From freshly caught seafood to mouthwatering pastries and gelato, Sorrento's food scene is a feast for the senses. Be sure to sample local specialties like limoncello, buffalo mozzarella, and sfogliatella, and don't hesitate to ask for recommendations from locals for the best places to dine. To make the most of your time in Sorrento, it's important to plan your visits to popular attractions strategically. Consider visiting major landmarks like the Amalfi Coast, Pompeii, and Capri during off-peak hours to avoid crowds and long lines. Additionally, booking guided tours in advance can help you maximize your time and gain valuable insights into the history and culture of the region.

Embrace the Magic of Sorrento's Evenings

As the sun sets over the Bay of Naples, Sorrento comes alive with an irresistible energy and charm. Spend your evenings sipping cocktails at waterfront bars, enjoying live music performances in Piazza Tasso, or dancing the night away at one of the city's vibrant nightclubs. Don't be afraid to let loose and immerse yourself in the magic of Sorrento's nightlife scene.

Stay Local and Support Small Businesses

When it comes to accommodations and dining options, consider staying at locally owned hotels and guesthouses and dining at family-run restaurants and trattorias. Not only will you enjoy a more authentic experience, but you'll also be supporting the local economy and preserving the unique character of Sorrento for future generations to enjoy.

Prepare for the Elements

Sorrento enjoys a Mediterranean climate characterized by hot summers and mild winters, but it's always wise to be prepared for changing weather conditions. Pack sunscreen, a hat, and sunglasses for protection against the sun, as well as a light jacket or sweater for cooler evenings. And don't forget to bring comfortable walking shoes for exploring the city's cobblestone streets.

Final Thoughts

As you prepare to embark on your journey to Sorrento, I hope these insider tips and recommendations will help you create unforgettable memories and experiences.

Whether you're savoring the flavors of Neapolitan cuisine, exploring ancient ruins, or simply basking in the beauty of Sorrento's coastal landscapes, may your time in this enchanting destination be filled with wonder, discovery, and joy. And remember, the true magic of Sorrento lies not only in its breathtaking scenery and historic landmarks but also in the warmth and hospitality of its people. So, come with an open heart and an adventurous spirit, and let Sorrento weave its spell on you, leaving you forever enchanted and longing to return. Safe travels, and may your journey be filled with moments of pure magic and delight.

SORRENTO TRAVEL PLANNER

NAME:
_____

DEPARTURE DATE:
_____

RETURN DATE:
_____

MY PACKING LIST

- _____
- _____
- _____
- _____
- _____
- _____
- _____
- _____
- _____
- _____
- _____

MY TRAVEL BUDGET

- _____
- _____
- _____
- _____
- _____
- _____
- _____
- _____
- _____
- _____
- _____
- _____
- _____
- _____
- _____
- _____
- _____
- _____

A-7 DAY TRAVEL ITINERARIES PLANNING

DAY 1:

DAY 2:

DAY 3:

DAY 4:

_____

_____

_____

DAY 5:

_____

_____

_____

DAY 6:

_____

_____

_____

DAY 7

_____

_____

_____

_____

MUST-DO THINGS IN SORRENTO

MUST-TRY FOOD IN SORRENTO

- _____
- _____
- _____
- _____
- _____
- _____
- _____
- _____
- _____
- _____
- _____
- _____
- _____
- _____

LIST OF TOURIST SITES & HIDDEN GEMS TO VISIT IN SORRENTO

SHARE YOUR SORRENTO TRAVEL EXPERIENCE

Printed in Great Britain
by Amazon